SPIRITUAL WISDOM FROM THE ALTAI MOUNTAINS
ALTAI BILIK

This book by an Altai scholar close to historical memory and source materials, is a valuable addition to our knowledge of Siberian culture and belief systems, illuminating the relatively unknown Altai White Faith – its concepts and specific language – in its relationship to nature, cosmic forces and the natural history of the human soul.

Eva Jane Neumann Fridman, **Ph.D.**, Author of *Sacred Geography*; co-editor: *Shamanism: an Encyclopedia of World Beliefs, Practices, and Culture.*

Of all of my travels on this planet I do not think any have moved me so deeply as my journey through Altai. I could not recommend this book highly enough. Altai *bilik* is knowledge of the human soul and the harmonious interweaving of human existence with greater cosmic reality. This book of timeless and universal wisdom is a necessary reminder to humanity as we prepare to enter the Noosphere, the next stage of our conscious evolution on Earth.

Jose Arguelles, Ph.D., Author of *The Mayan Factor* and *Manifesto for the Noosphere.*

A rare and lucid glimpse into an ancient cosmovision that may otherwise be forgotten. *Spiritual Wisdom of the Altai Mountains* presents meticulously translated spiritual principles, derived through academic as well as mystical means. It is a guide to enlightened society and prophesies a transition into an era of harmony foretold by diverse original cultures. A precious and dedicated piece of work that transcends time and culture.

Llyn Roberts, M.A., Director of Dream Change and author of *Shapeshifting into Higher Consciousness.*

Nikolai Shodoev's book *Spiritual Wisdom of the Altai* is a must for anyone who is interested in the mysticism of Siberia, past and present. Mr. Shodoev does a wonderful job of making his knowledge of religion and wisdom of his Altai people accessible to the Western reader.

Frederick Lundahl, Former US Foreign Service Officer and Specialist on Central Asia

Featuring the voice of elder Nikolai Shodoev, this book provides valuable insights into the shamanic worldviews of indigenous Altai peoples, using the concept of 'bilik' — folk wisdom.

Marjorie Mandelstam Balzer, Ph.D. Georgetown University, Editor of the Journal *Anthropology and Archeology of Eurasia* and the book *Shamanic Worlds*.

Spiritual Wisdom from the Altai Mountains
Altai Bilik

Spiritual Wisdom from the Altai Mountains
Altai Bilik

Nikolai Andreevich Shodoev

Translated by Joanna Dodson

MOON
BOOKS

Winchester, UK
Washington, USA

First published by Moon Books, 2012
Moon Books is an imprint of John Hunt Publishing Ltd., Laurel House, Station Approach,
Alresford, Hants, SO24 9JH, UK
office1@jhpbooks.net
www.johnhuntpublishing.com
www.moon-books.net

For distributor details and how to order please visit the 'Ordering' section on our website.

ISBN: 978 1 78099 121 4

Design: Stuart Davies

Originally published in Russian as 'Altai Bilik' co-authored by Nikolai Andreevich Shodoev
and Rustam Kurchakov, 'TAY', Kazan 2005. English translation, foreword and afterword
by Joanna Dobson.

Printed and bound by CPI Group (UK) Ltd, Croydon, CR0 4YY

We operate a distinctive and ethical publishing philosophy in all
areas of our business, from our global network of authors to
production and worldwide distribution.

CONTENTS

Introduction   1

Religion & the Bilik in Altai   5

Author's foreword   20

'Kangyi', Heaven and Earth,'   24

Spirituality and the Soul   36

Cycles   59

Altai Faith   73

Afterword   99

Significant Dates   102

Acknowledgment

Sincere thanks to Natalya Akchaevna Shodoeva, Director of the I.V Shodoev Local History Museum in Ust' Kan for her kindness and assistance with photographic material and the compilation of Nikolai Andreevich Shodoev's biography.

Introduction

I first met Nikolai Andreevich Shodoev at the Museum of Traditional Altai Culture in 2002. It quickly became apparent that Nikolai Andreevich is no ordinary museum worker. He took time to consider the nature of our group before accompanying us into the museum and beckoned us towards a *chakyr* — the wooden tying post that stands outside every *ail* — traditional Altai dwelling. The top was carved into the form of a horse's head and there were six indents carved out below it decorated with engraved geometric symbols. Nikolai Andreevich stood there beside the sturdy wooden pole that held the dimensions of the Altai worlds in place, a lean figure in a smart suit, and introduced himself and his work. He said that the diverse Turkic peoples of Altai shared a pool of traditional knowledge that he referred to as *bilik,* a Turkic word, the meaning of which encapsulates the notions of 'knowledge', 'science', 'cognition' and 'wisdom'. The exhibits we would see in the museum all represented different facets of *bilik*, this pool of traditional knowledge. As Nikolai Andreevich unlocked the heavy wooden museum door he looked back over his shoulder and told us to pay attention to any peculiar sensations we might experience as we entered the first room. He quietly muttered something in Altai as we crossed the threshold. We gathered in the corner of the museum room below the raised *dyiak* — altar, made of long, hanging white, blue and yellow pieces of cotton, surrounded by exhibits, detailed maps of the sky, illustrated pantheons and stone idols. Then, pointing to a diagram of curious symbols placed next to an old *kam's dyiak* our unusual museum guide began to describe how everything originated in spirit...

It was several years later that I met with Rustam Kurchakov who co-authored the Russian version of *Altai Bilik*. I was staying with an Altai family and being summer we sat in the ail around the fire. The family gradually joined us having completed their various chores, each making themselves comfortable on low wooden stools or the bed that stood in the men's half of the ail. Someone would feed the fire from time to time as it crackled or kept silence in response to the thoughts expressed there. Late into the evening, Rustam asked if I would translate *Altai Bilik* into English. As the smoke curled upwards I gave my word. Hardly could I have imagined that it would be as many years as there are walls to the *ail* or rungs to the tying post before the English version of '*Altai Bilik*' would finally make its way into print. Over the past six years, I have translated many texts into English on a variety of subject matter. Unlike any other translation however, it is the relatively few pages of *Spiritual Wisdom From The Altai Mountains: Altai Bilik* that have required all the experience of my years in Altai to complete. In the translation, I have particularly striven to retain the unique quality of Nikolai Andreevich's voice.

Much ethnographic material on the peoples of Altai exists in the Russian language. Some of the earliest ethnographic sketches occur in the travel journals of individuals who lead expeditions through the Altai in the nineteenth and early twentieth centuries such as the botanist V.V. Sapojhnikov and the German botanist A.A. Bunge. V.Verbitsky who represented the 'Altai Spiritual Mission' was one of the first to provide general descriptive ethnographic material and to document the Altai clan system. In the pre-revolutionary period V.V. Radlov travelled extensively in Altai publishing his famous work *Iz Sibiri* (*From Siberia*) and G.N. Potanin published *Materials on the History of Siberia* in 1867. The most authoritative ethnographic materials on shamanism in Altai are the works of L.P. Potapov including *Altaiskiy shamanizm* (*Altai Shamanism*, 1991) and A.V. Anokhin who studied the musical culture of the peoples of Altai. A.V. Anokhin wrote a number of research papers including *Materials on Altai Shamanism* (1924) and *Burkhanism in Western Altai* (1927). Almost all these researchers had the practice of including in their expeditions professional artists whose work captures endless tiny details of life, personal names, place names and the names of everyday objects. Of the many writers who have focused their attention on Burkhanism and the White Faith, particularly useful are *Taina Doliny Tereng* (*The mystery of the Tereng Valley*) by L. Sherstova (1997) and *Burkhanism, iz istorii natsional'no-osvoboditelnogo dvizheniia v Gornom Altae* (*Burkhanism, from the history of a national liberation movement in Gorny Altai*) by A.G. Danilin (1993).

There is currently little material concerning the Altai Republic and the indigenous peoples of the Altai published in English. *Siberia: A Record of Travel, Climbing, and Exploration* (1905) by Samuel Turner describes Turner's exploration of Mount Belukha situated in the South of the Altai Republic. Russian painter and thinker Nicholas Roerich did much to popularise the sacredness of the same mountain in *Altai-Himalaya: A Travel Diary*. A translation of the Altai epic poem *Maday-Qara* with an introduction and notes by Ugo Marazzi is available in addition to various articles and materials on the internet.

In setting a context for *Spiritual Wisdom From The Altai Mountains: Altai Bilik* it is important to emphasize that in writing about his own people and culture, Nikolai Andreevich Shodoev does what no other Russian or foreign researcher has attempted. Drawing on sources as varied as ancient rock art, Altai epic poems, myths, legend, the ethnographic sketches of Altai artist Choros-Gurkhin and the words of wisdom carriers, Nikolai Andreevich reaches into the depths of his cultural heritage seeking to piece together parts of a mosaic that form an unwritten philosophy, a pool of traditional knowledge. The material is unique partly on account of Nikolai Andreevich's own interpretative skills but also due to the input of those figures like A.G. Kalkhin, one of the last great shamanic figures in Altai. It was from Kalkhin that Nikolai Andreevich learned of the base-6 numeral system — *Enchi chak,* of the Moon's two invisible 'satellites' (epic heroes) and their role, and of the significance of the power of the new moon — *tom* and the power of the old moon — *om*.

The original introduction to the Russian version of *Altai Bilik* by Rustam Kurchakov is included here as Chapter One as it gives a useful overview of religion in the Altai. The text has been edited and explanatory notes added to assist the English speaking reader.

Joanna Dobson, 2011

A Note on Languages

All Altai words from the original text are shown in italics. Russian words are indicated in the text with explanatory notes.

Religion & the Bilik in Altai

"The creation of myth is the careful and unbiased observation of processes within the natural world that takes place over centuries. Myth-making is a way of parcelling strategic knowledge so that it can be transmitted through time to the era when it is most needed."

A.N. Dmitriev[1]

The Altai Republic is situated at the south of Siberia and shares borders with Mongolia, China and Kazakhstan. In the past, Altai served as a dynamic crossroads on the migration routes of ancient Asia, sustaining close ties with all the great empires and civilizations of Eurasia. Altai is the original homeland of more than thirty Turkic peoples who emigrated throughout Asia as along the branches of a huge tree.

In ancient times the word *Altai* referred to all the main mountain systems located at the heart of Asia, including the Himalayas, Karakorum and Sayan. To this day the notion of "twelve-faceted Kin-Altai" remains alive in folk memory. *Kin-Altai* translates as "Altai, navel of the Earth". This metaphor conveys the notion that Altai serves as one of the portals that connect the earth with the universe, providing nourishment to the planet just as a mother provides her child with essential nourishment via the umbilical cord.

The image of "twelve-faceted Kin-Altai," was later reduced to separate parts. Nonetheless, Altai remains a many faceted concept incorporating Gobi Altai, Mongolian Altai and Rudny Altai (Kazakhstan) as well as Russian Altai. At the heart of Asia, Altai is a key source of Asian spirituality; a cradle of religions. In the heart of the Altai indigenous people the ancient wisdom of rich historical memory has been preserved. Elder Nikolai Andreevich Shodoev refers to the Altai folk wisdom as *bilik*.

Bilik — A Dynamic Worldview

The *bilik* can be described as a contemporary myth that abides in the soul of the Altai people, endowing them with a holistic worldview. It is a myth that is constantly evolving. It simultaneously incorporates ancient wisdom while embracing contemporary science. The content of the *bilik* is constantly being re-assimilated philosophically and serves as a prism, through which solutions to contemporary problems may be found.

The *bilik* has been preserved by the contemporary Altai people, at least in its most essential form. It is an ancient, sacred treasure that has been passed from one generation to another in the forms of history, oral culture and behavioural codes. Until now, it has existed in the memory of the Altai people, their traditions, customs and views but not in written form.

Aspects of the *bilik* have also been preserved in cultural monuments, museum exhibits, religious symbols and rock carvings. Myths and legends continue to live in the minds of the older and the younger generations, not yet having being consigned to the category of lifeless, literary monument.

The *bilik* embodies a very particular perception of the universe, nature and human society, drawing on the collective experience of centuries. It reveals a profound relationship to life, a deep understanding of natural energies and rhythms and a keen feeling for the dramatic contradictions of our time.

The Altai word *bilik* conveys the meaning of the words *knowledge, cognition, wisdom* and *science (N.A. Baskakov, T.M.Toshakova. Oirotsko-russkii slovar. Izd.Mosckva 1947 pp.31).* With the separation of rational science from common, holistic knowledge the word *bilik* was gradually replaced by *bilim.* The suffix *-im* in the Altai language is used as a third person plural verb ending and so *bilim* conveys the sense that the *bilik* is linked with action and with "doing."

Knowledge encapsulated in the *bilik* includes Altai knowledge

going back to the times of the atlases (*Sartakpa*[2] and other mythological heroes) and extending to the present day. Contemporary
research has shown that the ancient Altai people had different
types of knowledge such as: written language — *yjyk bichik*
(rhunic script), *tekpe bichik* (from the times of Oirot-Khan[3]), *todo
bichik* (mathematics), zoology (main activities were animal
husbandry and hunting), botanics (the use of plants for food,
healing, ritual purposes, dwelling construction), geology and
minerology (knowledge of ores and smelting).

Wisdom they say, directs a person only towards beneficial
actions. Of wisdom it is said that a person who knows and
observes the laws of nature, who respects and lives in harmony
with the forces of nature is a wise person, for man, animals and
inert objects all exist within the world of 'nature'. They are all
interconnected and dependent on the power and energy of the
sky, fire and water (spirits). A wise person agrees all their actions
with higher powers, with God (*Kuda*[4]), the angels (*keteeler),* with
the spirits of the mountains, rivers and springs (*ak eeler*) and with
the spirits of the ancestral home (*ak tostor Jajhil-Kan, Bakty-Kan*).
A wise man addresses the spirits and requests protection for the
people, particularly for children from dark forces, illness and
death. A.G. Kalkin[5], the shaman and 'master of Altai *Kai*[6]
singing' is said to have been one of these people.

Unity of faith and knowledge

The *bilik* is an integral, folk ideology, in which knowledge and
faith are indivisibly linked. The *bilik* is not limited by strict
canons or religious dogma, as they simply don't exist in the Altai
faith in the common sense of the word. This is a faith that draws
on the historical experience of the people, embraces contemporary scientific knowledge, and is unusual in its pragmatism.
Faith for the Altai people must above all else be practical and
applicable to life's most demanding problems.

Turning to the power of the heavens and to the world of spirit is something that an Altai person does throughout their whole life, be it at the point of marriage, the birth of a child, significant stages of one's children's upbringing or at the completion of one's own journey through life. Individual, direct communication with higher powers is considered a powerful source of life force.

In turn, knowledge is expected to be spiritually oriented and so draws on faith. The limitations of purely rational thinking are acknowledged for it is held that certain higher truths exist which are inaccessible to the rational mind being made conscious through the heart or soul only. Such knowledge becomes wisdom and serves as a genuine source of strength and support.

Within the understanding of the *bilik*, knowledge and faith share the same source: the unity of common laws pertaining to the universe, nature and man. Despite being just a tiny particle in the world, man nonetheless reflects all the energies and rhythms of the earth, sun and universe in his soul, intellect and body.

The *bilik* mainly contains strategic knowledge concerning the relationship between man and the cosmos. It contains an understanding of the essential foundation of being; the laws of creation and the development of the world. One's life purpose, fate, the laws of interaction between human beings, the laws of harmony and love are all encompassed in the *bilik*.

Another distinctive feature of the *bilik* is that it represents collective knowledge. The acceptance that every individual has their own truth and knowledge in accordance with their own unique destiny is a common characteristic of the Altai faith. It is believed that every individual carries and develops a particular aspect of knowledge throughout their life. As a result, the people collectively maintain the treasure of wisdom in its entirety.

The core of the *bilik* lies in sacred knowledge. It is neither overtly exhibited nor is it fixed in one particular source. The Eastern proverb has it that, "he who knows, does not speak and he who speaks, does not know." The equivalent Altai proverb translates as: "He who knows speaks one wise word. He who does not know speaks a thousand words." Not everything may be expressed in words, and one and the same thing may be expressed in different ways using different words. The external, symbolic side of the *bilik* is quite accessible, taking the form of myth, legend, heroic tales, cult signs, ceremonies, *alkyshak* (blessings), and everyday customs. However, the profound and essential knowledge of the *bilik* can only be grasped in its entirety by the heart. The Altai people themselves are not given to speaking of the sacred. They carry it silently in the "centre of the soul," at the "heart of the heart."

Above all, the *bilik* serves self-awareness and development of the soul. It focuses on a person's self-development, irrespective of social position, nationality, or religion. Every step on the path of acquiring such knowledge involves true spiritual experience and represents a genuine act of creation.

The *bilik* gives one to understand that man, being in intimate relationship with the world has from the very outset been given all the knowledge and treasures of the world by Nature herself. This knowledge is to be found at the centre of the soul.

The *bilik* concentrates largely on the soul, its heavenly origin and different states and stages of development. The *bilik* attributes the creation of the soul centre to *cosmic* energies and points to the soul centre as the source of energy that determines a person's fate, life purpose, and power of thought.

It is the soul centre, the place where heart and mind meet, that is the great keeper of wisdom. It is here that one forms the image of one's environment and worldview. It is said that the *bilik* opens up the alga rhythms of a person's inner, spiritual working, converting knowledge into life force.

This is the Altai indigenous understanding of true, complete knowledge. In all other matters the *bilik* gravitates towards knowledge currently being developed by science. The *bilik* remains receptive to other cultures and traditions.

Faith

"Asia is a cradle of religions. Altai is the heart and soul of Asia." (from the Roerich legacy[7])

The essence of the Altai faith is based on conscious spirituality, direct, personal communication with the Sky. It is essentially a faith in kindness, in the light essence of life and in the existence of higher powers that determine the laws common to every living being. It is a belief in the power of individual spirit and purpose. It is love for the world, for others and a striving towards beauty and harmony in all things.

The power of this faith lies both in the natural world and in the people. For the Altai people, God takes the form of nature, on which they depend and of which they are an integral part. The Altai faith developed from an animistic worldview. It continues to develop, retaining its foundation in folk wisdom while taking account of changing historical conditions. In every epoch, the Altai faith has reflected the spiritual laws of the subtle worlds accessible to man. These perceptions are subtle and change with the times; they are reflected in myth, legend and ritual.

At the current time there is no universal name for the Altai faith. The Altai people themselves refer to their faith differently. Faith in the blue sky above is called *Tengriism* (*tengre d'ang*), but other branches of faith in the Altai include *White Faith* (*Ak d'ang*)[8], *Burkhanism*[9], and shamanism. It is diverse in its perception of the Highest and peculiarities of ritual.

Ak Jang - 'White Faith'

Over the course of history the ancestors of the Altai people came into close contact with different religions and belief systems. Seperate Altai tribes were familiar with Nestorian Christianity even during the time of Genghis Khan. Christian motifs strengthened towards the end of the nineteen century as part of the population became baptized. Lamaist Buddhism was the official state religion in the seventeenth and eighteenth centuries during the period of the inclusion of the Altai tribes in the Oirot Khanate. Islam was the religion of the Turkic neighbours, in particular, the Kazakh. Shamanism however, which included worship of Tengeri, Ier-Suu and Umai-Ene was the Altai people's own religious system. It embraced the teaching of the three worlds and was divided into white and black shamanism.

It was white shamanism (associated with good spirits) that was chosen as the foundation for religious renewal in the early twentieth century and called the 'White Faith'. Advocates of 'Ak Jang' ruled out contact with the dark spirits and the underworld, having proclaimed worship to the white guardians only. The highest deity was recognised as Altai-Kudai (Ak Burkhan) in place of Ulgen and the name 'spirits of place' was replaced by 'burkhans'. This explains the second name for the White Faith, 'burkhanism'. Certain deities from the lamaist pantheon of the Oirot Khanate reclaimed their niche, widening the circle of shamanic spirits or co-existing alongside them. Blood sacrifice to the spirits using cattle was stopped and the use of wine and tobacco in rituals became prohibited. Advocates of the White Faith were called 'jarlykchi' (messenger). Sometimes shamans became jarlykchi if they accepted the renewal of the faith. At the beginning of the twentieth century White Faith served as a stimulus for the ethnic unity of the Altai people and represents the experience of their religious unity.

Altai — A Cultural Treasure, NII Tsentr, Moscow, 2004

The Altai faith clearly reflects individual free will, personal independence and responsibility before the eternal laws of life, nature and one's fellow men.

It is accepted that every individual has their own God and every soul is holy because one's fate and purpose are determined by heaven.

The Altai faith cannot perhaps be called a "religion" in the strictest sense of the word. It defies formal, academic classification. Monotheism, paganism, pantheism, magic, shamanism and even elements of totemism are intricately intertwined within the one faith. Refusing any form of canonization, the Altai faith has maintained its distinctive origins, despite considerable pressure from representatives of Buddhism (Lamaism) and Christianity.

As far as one might judge from history, the Altai faith has remained free of political manipulation. On the contrary, various leaders of the great Turkic empire are recorded as having drawn their spiritual strength from it.

Due to the different religions and cults that came to Altai with the constant shifting of peoples and tribes, Altai has for centuries seen the co-existence of different belief systems that have inevitably played their part in influencing and expanding the spiritual practice and mythology of the indigenous population.

From the Middle Ages onward, however, Altai has experienced quite considerable direct pressure and oppression from missionaries of various "world religions" and religious groups.

The Altai faith can be said to be based on four key belief systems: *Tengriism*: belief in the One Sky God, '*Kek Tengri*'; *Worship of the spirits of Nature*: a unique Altai pantheism and deification of Nature; *Ancestral* worship and the *White Faith* - worship of the one heavenly God, the White Burkhan and the expected return of the Oirot-khan as a national hero and Savior.

All these systems were closely linked and ultimately enrich each other. The dominant ideas and peculiarities of cults and rituals were determined by the historical conditions of the lives of the Altai people. Attributing spirituality and intelligent powers to nature and preserving an intimate, 'krovnoi', ('krov' Russian meaning '*blood*') relationship with her has remained the most constant element of the Altai faith in its entirety.

The notion of the Eternal Sky as the one God originated with the Turkic and Mongol peoples of Asia in ancient times, long before the acceptance and canonization of "world religions." According to historian L.N. Gumilev,[10] the ancient Tengriians worshipped the sunlight. Tengriism served as the spiritual basis of the Turkic culture and state for a period of nearly two thousand years up until the fourteenth century.

Tengriism

Tengeri' is the name of the Sky Deity also called *'Ten-eri-kudai'* - 'Sky God', *'Kek Ten-eri'* - Blue Sky, and *'Men-kyu Ten-eri'* - 'Eternal Sky'. Among the Central Asian nomadic peoples, worship of the Sky God *Tengeri* dates back to as early as the Hunnish period. It was believed that the Sky not only gifted life to each and every individual but also gave the state to a people and supreme power to the Kagan. The khans of Turkic states before the Middle Ages based their power on a mandate from *Tengeri,* presenting themselves as sons of *Tengeri* and his representatives on earth. A ruler reigned under Tengeri's protection for as long as he was in accord with the laws of Heaven. If he ruled improperly *Tengeri* withdrew his support, and the ruler either perished or fell from power.

At the present time elements of the sky worship can still be witnessed in ritual practice. At collective prayer meetings when the 'Eulogy to Altai' is performed the people address the Blue Sky along with other deities and spirits of the sacred mountains.

When the strips of cotton (*jalama* and *kyira*) are tied to the boughs of a larch as an offering to the gods and spirits among them, a separate strip is dedicated to the Blue Sky. When libation is carried out with milk, the name *Kek Tengeri* is pronounced first and only then followed by *Altai-Kudai,* the spirits of the mountains and rivers, names of birds and animals.

Worship of the ancient Sky God *Tengeri* has a significant place in the rich tapestry of the spiritual worldview of the contemporary Altai people. There are also modern movements to revive Tengriism, particularly in respect to living in harmony with natural forces and caring for the earth.

Altai — A Cultural Treasure, NII Tsentr, Moscow, 2004

Alongside Tengriism, shamanism was also practiced and involved communication with spirit for the purposes of healing the sick and soothing the souls of the deceased. L.N. Gumilev suggests that shamanism in Altai experiences a renewal over intervals of between seven and twelve centuries. In ancient times, the word *kam* referred to a person who could reach into other worlds and communicate with the spirits. Among *kams*, one would find tellers, musicians, seers and healers.

After the fall of the Great Turkic Empire, memory of *Tengeri* as the highest deity continues to be evident. However, ancestral and local deities emerge as being more prominent after the fall of the Empire. Subsequently, every tribe had its own *Altai*, its own Guardian, progenitor and provider.

In the middle ages, the word *Tengeri* often gave way to the Persian name *Kudai* and later became equated with the Christian god. Nonetheless, Tengriism resisted assimilation despite missionary activity and has been preserved to this day.

When Tengriism lost its status as state religion, the significance of shamanic cults grew. Rather than focusing on the one God shamanism focuses on the mystical teachings of nature, the spirits of nature and ancestral spirit. Shamanism in Altai adapted to the existing belief system and created the cult of *Ulgen* as the supreme deity and creator of life on earth. In Altai myth *Ulgen's* brother *Erlik* is said to be the keeper of the underworld. Correspondingly, shamans who fulfilled the role of mediator between the upper and lower worlds were either "white" which meant that they served *Ulgen*, or "black" which meant that they served *Erlik*.

During the Oirot rule, White Faith began to distance itself from black shamanism, animal sacrifice, and co-operation with dark spirits. After Altai joined Russia in the eighteenth century, folk beliefs were forced "underground" as a result of force on the part of Christian missionaries. It became a hidden faith and began the process of adapting to new conditions of economic and spiritual colonization. However, at the very beginning of the twentieth century, *Ak dyang*, (White Faith or Burkhanism) underwent a resurgence in the form of a new national religion in counterbalance to shamanism, which had become outmoded. White Faith is, above all else, aimed at generating kindness and grace among the people. In Altai, Burkhanism has become a movement of religious reform, but has not as yet been formalized into the religious system. The Burkhanist movement is viewed with understanding and sympathy by the democratic Russian intelligentsia but was immediately rejected and crushed by reactionary forces from the "Altai Spiritual Mission," a nationalist organization run by Russian immigrants, and was equally unsupported by local administrative bodies. For different reasons White Believers were also made subject to persecution and repression in the nineteen twenties and thirties.

It is curious that, in all the different belief systems prevalent in Altai Tengriism, shamanism, and White Faith, it is the pantheon of Nature spirits that remains the one essentially consistent aspect. The key pantheon consists of:

- The spirit of the homeland - one's personal, ancestral Altai with its sacred mountain, valley, animal, and ancestral tree;
- The spirit of the main elements of Earth, Water, Fire, etc.;
- The guardian of place - guardian of the mountain, forest, springs, home, path, etc.;
- Gods and Burkhans from the heavenly and earthly realms.

Many would describe the bubbling cauldron of the Altai faith as capable of bringing forth and uniting that which would otherwise be totally incompatible. Many ideas and notions originating from faiths external to the indigenous world, even those forcibly imposed, are ultimately simmered away in the cauldron until they eventually become an organic part of the native belief system.

How can monotheism and a hierarchy of Gods and burkhans coexist in one belief system? How can one explain that *Tengeri*, *Ulgen*, and *Kangyi* (who is by legend the son of *Ulgen*) all hold the status of Highest deity? What is the essential idea at the root of the notion that *Erlik* (guardian of the underworld, younger brother of *Ulgen*) plays a more active and practical role in the creation of life on earth than *Ulgen* himself? (According to myth, *Ulgen*, having completed the act of creation, fell asleep in the distant heavens to awaken only at the advent of the "white era.")

Every Altai clan has its own peculiarities and perceptions of gods, spirits, legends, myths, and rituals; and one can easily point to contradictions in the interpretation of belief. This is not necessarily a sign of weakness or backwardness. Rather it is the inevitable characteristic of a dynamic faith that is constantly adapting and evolving. Its seemingly archaic quality at times reveals itself to be highly contemporary and timely, emphasizing the freedom of human spirit, the connectedness of all living things and all parts of the Universe, the relativity of concepts of good and evil, and spirituality in the relationship between man and the natural world.

The freedom of the Altai faith from strict canons and logical systematization illustrates its openness to the changes of the contemporary world and to other religions and beliefs, traditions, and cultures.

The purpose of this book is to give the reader a preliminary sense of an indigenous knowledge that is both ancient and contemporary. This knowledge can only be truly received by an open heart.

I am deeply grateful to Nikolai Andreevich for the opportunity to have touched on the secrets of the *bilik*. I am sure that we, as representatives of the great peoples of Russia, shall benefit from the rejuvenation of our ancient, spiritual source. My modest role in the preparation of the Russian version of this material on the *bilik* has been as *"tilmeshchi"* (translator). Although the main ideas and concepts are given here in translation, this should not prevent the reader from attempting to feel the indigenous meaning and sounds of the Altai words and the resonance of their inner energy. Unfortunately, in today's world this is a rare ability.

It is possible that members of the Altai community will disagree with some of the interpretations offered in this book. As has already been said, however, one of the main characteristics of the Altai worldview is its diversity and the acknowledgement of the right of each and every individual to his or her own vision of life. Academics may also view some aspects of the *bilik* with scepticism, in response to which I would emphasize that this book is not an academic work, but rather an attempt to make the foundation of an ancient and dynamic form of wisdom more widely available.

May *Kek-Tengri* and *Kan Altai*, Eternal Sky and Sacred Altai remain forever blessed! *Rustam Kurchakov (edited by Joanna Dobson)*

Elder and Author Nikolai Andreevich Shodoev

Nikolai Andreevich Shodoev is a well known figure both throughout Altai and beyond. He was born in 1934 in the village of Ust' Kan, Altai Republic. Like most children of the war years Nikolai learned the responsibility of hard work and from the age of twelve began replacing those who had left for the front working in the Kolkhoz or helping out herding sheep and calves.

During the winter nights of the war years Nikolai and the other children would listen to Altai epic tales *"Altai Baatylar"* by N.U. Ulagashev and when playing the boys would pretend to be one of the heroes from the epic tales. Nikolai loved to listen to the historical myths and legends told to him by his grandmother Temesh Shodoeva whilst herding cattle together at the Kolkhoz. Hence, Nikolai first became acquainted with the foundation of the *bilik* in his childhood.

Nikolai Shodoev worked as a history teacher and then head of the Mendur Sokkon village school in the Ust' Kan region. In the seventies, collecting material on local history and then the *Bilik* became a hobby and gradually, his life's work. In 1986 Nikolai Andreevich opened the Mendur Sokkon local history museum 'The Museum of Traditional Altai Culture', which in 1994 became formally affiliated to the Republic's A.V. Anokhin[11] Museum. In 2007, the Museum of Traditional Altai culture was officially relocated to the centre of the Ust' Khan region. The building in Mendur Sokkon continues to function as a visitors' centre for those interested in the Altai spiritual culture and has been renamed 'Museum of Altai Spiritual Culture'.

N.A. Shodoev is the author of three fictional works inspired by the motifs of Altai myth and legend. He has also written more than ninety articles in which various contemporary problems are viewed through the prism of the *bilik*. Among the Altai people, there are those who say that Shodoev has *"sudurom"*, which is a mythical, secret knowledge of the book of wisdom often referred to in Altai legends and sagas.

Nikolai Andreevich reads the history and ancient knowledge of Altai in cult signs, in half-forgotten native words, many of which have since disappeared from contemporary use, in myths and legends, in the skies, in artefacts in his museum, and in stories told by Altai elders and clairvoyants.

Nikolai Andreevich continues his work on the *bilik* which includes: re-assimilating the history of Altai and the intertwining of the historical fates of Altai and Russia; defining perceptions of the cosmos; the calendar system; the peculiarities of calendar making; the laws of soul development; achieving a condition of harmony in our troubled time and the transition from the "yellow" to the "white" era.

Author's foreword

Visitors to the museum in Mendur Sokkon, tourists and researchers alike, are always curious to know where I sourced the ancient knowledge and historical information that has accumulated during my work on the *bilik*. Here, in this short introduction to the *Altai Bilik*, I attempt to answer this question. Altai epic literature such as *Altai Baatyrlar* (Altai epic heroes) in expositions by N.U. Ulagasheva[12], A.G. Kalkin, and other folk tellers served as key sources. These individuals were more than knowledge keepers, singers, or tellers. They were also healers and prophets who with their ability to communicate with the other world, (*ol d'er*), helped people with day-to-day problems such as finding lost cattle or a stolen item, healing the sick, and giving advice or blessing.

The ethnographic sketches of the first Altai artist and public figure G.E. Choros-Gurkin provided another important source. Albums of his work are held at the A.V. Anokhin Local History Museum in Gorno-Altaisk. These sources had to be "deciphered" as the knowledge and information they contain is presented allegorically, in image form, and often hinted at only.

I learned much from the Altai myths and legends told to me as a child by my *Kargan-ene* (Grandmother) Temesh Shodoeva. Later, important information on specific matters was obtained from conversations held with *jarlykchi*[13] (clairvoyants and others with extrasensory skills): T.M. Klesheva, K.M. Kipchakova, Y.K. Megedekovy, E.M. Chebotareva, M.S. Golubeva, and others. Much helpful information has also been passed to me by my fellow countrywoman, Altai clairvoyant and healer Aradzhan Adunova.

Unhurried conversations held in high mountain meadows where shepherds watch their flocks in summer also come to mind.

These high meadows are unusual places where one can feel at one with nature and experience the effect of the meadows' particular energies. This type of environment lends itself to the telling of stories and reminiscence. One may hear legends, historical events retold, old parables and examples of ancient wisdom. Even young people become wiser from being in such an environment, becoming more independent in their judgment and actions. To shepherd high up in the mountains is of course work, but pleasant work nonetheless, giving time for long, in-depth conversation that develops into discussion and debate, one theme giving way to another. Sometimes, in such an atmosphere a person receives unexpected knowledge, a new view on life or experiences certain feelings for the first time. Many such conversations, put to one side in my mind, were recalled and reflected upon at a later date.

Fragments of collected folk wisdom have been compared with the content of both fictional and scientific literature and material taught both in schools and universities. In this way the systematization of the *bilik* took shape. Sometimes, even a previously unknown word or line of a song heard during prayer would jolt me into making a sudden realization. The Taigian Hunter's song (one hundred to one hundred and fifty years old) serves as one such example:

Тенгерининг судазын Кудай ден бодоган.
Телекейдинг аргазын кююним деп санангам.
I thought the heavenly axis was God, but I was wrong.
I hoped civilization would bring well being, but that was a lie.
(Heavenly axis: axis of the world, Milky Way; see chapter 'Kangyi, Heaven and Earth'.)

As a rule shamans do not reveal or explain sacred knowledge and so I was often required to "decode" new, or rather ancient but subsequently forgotten, words or principles spoken by shamans or *jarlykchi* by turning to other sources.

The folk *bilik* (knowledge, wisdom) encompasses all the branches of scientific knowledge required by a people to live on a given territory. The *bilik* paves the way for the material and spiritual development of that people. I am neither shaman nor *jarlykchi*. Rather, I consider the *bilik* to be folk wisdom, accumulated over many centuries. Much of what the *bilik* communicates is connected with the understanding of *ee* (spirit), *tyn* (soul), *Kudai* (God), and other mystical ideas concerning the subtle planes, and which in more contemporary language would be expressed as those energies (*D'imu*) which permeate the universe, which come from the earth and which surround a human being. Knowledge of this sort is related to folk wisdom rather than to religion. Ancient knowledge is often hidden behind religious or mystical concepts. It is the quintessential meaning behind these concepts that is the common element of any folk *bilik*.

The spiritual significance of the *bilik* is revealed through "White Faith." This faith is nonpolitical, neither is it a religion nor a primitive form of paganism, as it is sometimes depicted. White Faith is the knowledge that is found in the original sources of nature and society that are one for every individual irrespective of nationality, religion or education. It is an understanding of spiritual unity and the laws and phenomena of the universe that influence man as much as all other living beings on this earth.

White Faith guides one towards kindness and the light and has the potential to reveal the path to a more enlightened society — protecting mankind from social, natural, and other disasters if only it were tended patiently and cared for as the flower of all life. (The peony is a symbol representing all that is light and good in life.)

I am grateful to my associates in Altai, Kazan and Moscow, who helped in preparing this book for publication and became co-authors of the Russian version of *Altai Bilik*. I send them my warmest blessing.

My work on the *bilik* has continued over the years due to the constant care, support, and practical advice of my partner

Alexandra Grigorievna. I thank her with all my soul!

N.A. Shodoev, Mendur Sokkon, Altai Republic

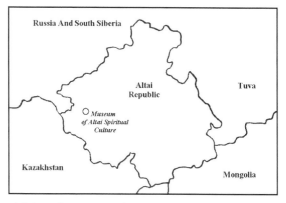

Figure 1. Map of Museum of Altai Spiritual Culture in the Altai Republic

A. Museum in Mendur Sokkon by Jodi Frediani. B. Shodoev with exhibits at the Museum of Altai Spiritual Culture by Jodi Frediani.

C. Rock art sanctuary in Altai by Joanna Dobson.

D. Aleksei Kalkhin (source Institute of Altai Studies Archive)

'Kangyi', Heaven and earth

"In the beginning there was the blue sky above and the dark earth below and between them — humanity's child." Orkhon Rhunic Inscription, Mongolia

Kangyi represents the most central and enigmatic principle within *bilik* cosmology. It is a manifestation of the highest, that which would normally be referred to as "the universe," "the cosmos." *Kangyi* gives the world structure and defines man's place within it. It is the ultimate, limitless, unknowable, living, all-hearing and all-seeing High Spirit; higher than any other god, for gods are many, whereas *Kangyi* is one and whole.

Finding a Russian equivalent for the word poses quite a problem, not so much due to a lack of linguistic material but rather due to a difference in worldview. The etymology of the sound and inner meaning of the word denotes: "most vital, most pure," "treasure of all treasures," "most holy of holy."

The "body" *Kangyi* embraces the galaxy. Its axis is the Milky Way and it runs from the North star (in Altai, *Altyn kasyk,* meaning "golden stake") through the sun and the planet earth and then protrudes outwards to one side (see figure 2). *Kangyi* is in constant motion along and around its axis. It rotates, swings like a pendulum and sways, "attached" to the "golden stake" of the polar star. On earth, this is said to be the "spirit of the Noosphere[14]."

Among the exhibits of the Mendur Sokkon Local History Museum (Ust' Kan region, Altai Republic) lies a symbolic representation of *Kangyi* in the form of a "World Egg" chiseled into stone. The undulating surface symbolizes the rotation of the stars and planets around *Kangyi*, the axis.

Kangyi is the living essence that sees, hears, feels, and is possessed of huge energetic power. It defines the structure and development of the three realms of Heaven, Earth, and the Underworld. In *Kangyi*, all types of vital energy are united, and it is from *Kangyi* that the human soul and other living beings are born.

In contrast to the visible world, *Kangyi* is the subtle world, the parallel world or *ol dyer* — the "other world." Its defining features are invisibility, intangible density, and the ability to permeate anywhere and everywhere.

It is supposed that the concept of the *ether,* referred to in esoteric and philosophical literature such as the works of Blavatsky, is kindred to the understanding of *Kangyi* contained within the *bilik.*

Contemporary physics has renamed the ancient concept of the ether the "physical vacuum." Novosibirsk academic A.N. Dmitriev writes, "This is etheric material, which, from the point of view of contemporary science, is the interactive medium for

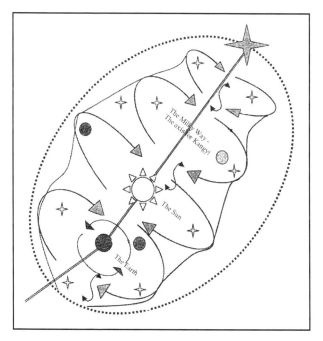

Figure 2. "World Egg" (the "body" *Kangyi*)

electric, magnetic, gravitational, and rotational fields. Etheric material, or the "physical vacuum" in the terms of contemporary physics, is present in every point of universal space and permeates all living and mineral beings. It is the common material of man and cosmic space. The qualities and potential of this subtle, etheric material have long been acknowledged and indeed applied by highly sensitive individuals, those with skills that have come to be referred to as extrasensory perception." (A.N. Dmitriev. *Fiery recreation of the earth's climate*. Novosibirsk, 2002, pp. 17-19)

Further characterizing the peculiarities of the present level of transformation of cosmic and earthly energies, Professor Dmitriev points to the existence of "some common, life-giving and information-giving energy that is present throughout the whole universe, every process and object. In addition it fills our every thought, feeling and action. This energy is the life source of every substance and all that exists either in reality or as potential. In the form of pure energy, it exists in every point of space and can be interpreted as potential fire that may be called to manifestation given the observance of required conditions. That call of energy is thought and emotion. Lightning and earthquakes represent the same phenomena.

"The current understanding of the 'physical vacuum' involves an omnipresent but unmanifest energy which is potential fire. Beyond potential fire lies its potential source. In the Bible it is written: 'God is the fire…'" (Dmitriev, pp. 108-110)

According to the *bilik*, life on earth has a cosmic origin linked with the influence of the subtle worlds on nature and human consciousness. The life forms known to us are born and develop as a result of interaction between heavenly (cosmic) and earthly energies, the paternal and maternal essence.

In the stories of the *ailatkyshchi* (Altai folk philosophers — keepers of antiquity) the stars and planets are living beings that communicate with each other exchanging energies either in harmony or in enmity with one another. Amongst them the earth is the cradle of life for it is from her depths that the energies of the cycles of Nature emerge accounting for the birth and development of all the diversity of man and the plant and animal kingdoms.

The *maternal energies* are those invisible energies or rays (*chok d'ymu*) that radiate from the earth's seven layers and are referred to as *ilbi, abi (albi), d'elbi and chydu*. (In Altai myth these maternal energies are called *mazha*. Renowned storyteller A.G. Kalkyn refers to them as *Keerkyui — Baraan —* "my sweet companion.")

Ilbi are the positive, life-confirming energies of all that is good. *Abi (albi)* are the negative energies associated with danger and misfortune. *D'elbi* are changeable, ambivalent energies, capable of creating good or evil depending on specific circumstances. *Chydu* is a strengthening energy that intensifies the potency of either of the energies mentioned above. These energies form the maternal life essence *ene-tyn* (maternal soul) or *ene-kyn* (navel, essence, root).

The paternal energies and life essence originate in cosmic light energies (*tot dymu* or *darkyn*). These energies penetrate to the earth's surface primarily from the Sun, stars, and planets. They are referred to as *ilbissin* (positive energies or rays of kindness), *abyssyn* (negative energies of danger and misfortune), *d'elbissin* (ambivalent energies), and *chirdirman* (intensifying energies). These are referred to collectively as *d'ymyrul* and make up the paternal essence *ada-tyn* (paternal soul) or *ada-kin* (paternal essence, root).

Anyone who has retained their connection with Nature is capable of feeling these earthly and cosmic energies. They can manifest as a rush of energy, a sudden realization, inexplicable feelings of happiness, or perhaps troubled unease at sunrise, beneath a starry sky, in a mountain landscape, flowering meadow, or beside a bubbling spring. It seems that contemporary civilization and city life stifle this ability for interaction, separating man from his natural 'pupovina' (Russian meaning navel). The ability to perceive or to feel the living energies of the earth and sky with the heart is most clearly apparent in children. Of course, there are also many individuals who display heightened sensitivity to these energies, such as clairvoyants and those with extrasensory abilities.

Powerful *jarlykchi* (clairvoyants, those who serve the Altai White Faith) feel, "see," and differentiate between manifestations of earth and cosmic energies. Places of high altitude, such as mountains, where positive energies (*ilbi, chydu*) are discharged and pulsate above the earth are considered sacred (*agaru, bailu*). It is these places that are chosen for public prayer. In Altai white ribbons called *kyira* are tied to the boughs of trees and milk is sprinkled on the ground. People go to sacred places to cleanse their aura, recharge with positive energy, and rid themselves of negative thoughts and feelings. It has been noted that in such places horses sniff the ground and roll in the grass gathering energy and strengthening their tired bodies.

In contrast, in places of low altitude where *abi* (*albi*), (rays of evil/misfortune) or *delbi* (ambivalent rays) are exuded, Altaians usually carry out the ritual of *kropleniya*, sprinkling *araka* (alcoholic drink from milk) to appease evil spirits on the traveler's journey in the sense of, "take this, be satisfied, and leave us be."

It has been known in such a place, for an evil spirit to stop a rider's horse, preventing him from going any further. To move on quickly, the rider lifts his horse's hooves and lights a fire under them, either with matches or a flint. In the absence of fire, riders have been known to wait until dawn before being able to continue their journey.

The natural world in Altai is permeated with powerful energetic currents, the effect of which is reflected in one way or another in the consciousness of the local inhabitants and fixed in the memory of generations in the form of customs, codes of behavior, myths, and legends. Every area has its sacred mountain (*bailu tuu*), river valley, sacred spring (*arzhan suu*), secret places and burial grounds. In the mountains, on plains, and in river valleys, there are hollows or craters with very powerful energy called *oibok or oibong*. Sometimes rituals are carried out in these places and public prayer meetings are held. Local people appeal to tourists and visitors for discretion and self-restraint and to observe certain codes of behavior when visiting such places. An ill-considered approach to natural energies can cause harm to a person and their health.

Places with powerful light energy can be found all over the world and they undoubtedly possess a strong magnetic quality. On a planetary scale, Gorny Altai is a place of great significance. In the *bilik* the profound meaning of the word *Altai* is given as "my God" or "my sacred impulses." With good reason it is referred to as *Kan Altai* (blood, our Altai), and also as *Kin-Altai* (female navel of the earth). Within the greater complex of our planet, Altai fulfills the role of a specific energetic matrix, a particular channel, the "umbilical cord," providing a link between the earth and the cosmos.

According to Altai cosmology *Kangyi's* "axis" stretches from the polar star via the sun through the heart of the earth, Kan Altai. It is depicted in the form of a tree trunk with its branches extending over Altai and the whole of Asia. In these sacred places (*bailu d'er*), a highly intense exchange of energies takes place between Mother Earth and Father Sky. In the Kosh-Agach region, there is a hollow that the local people call *D'erding Kini*, which translates as "navel of the earth." Places as sacred as these are many, not only in Altai but in Khakassia, Gorny shorya, and Kyrgyzstan.

When the paternal and maternal energies unite and merge, a synchronisation takes place resulting in the pulsation of different types of energy both subtle and more dense. This interaction is constantly taking place in what are referred to as the "*chaiykam*" (the eight heavenly vaults, the eight firmaments surrounding the globe).

In *bilik* cosmology the interplay of the two quintessential essences that is constantly giving birth to the diversity of earthly life is linked with the mythical images *Kek* and *Ak*. *Kek* means "blue" and in this context is understood as 'heavenly cosmic spirit'. (In Russian, the word heavenly comes from the root word for *sky,* hence the association with the colour blue.) *Ak* translates as "white" or as "the white of the eye or an egg," and represents the spirit of the corporeal, the spirit of the earth's four material elements and the spirit of earthly substance. This is how birth and reproduction occurs. Two pairs of cosmic essence function in the space of *Kangyi*. They are the Blue Creator and the White Creator (*Kek Dzhaiaan* and *Ak Dzhaiaan*) and the Blue and White Incarnator (*Kek Solon* and *Ak Solon*).

The Blue Creator is situated on the *Kangyi* axis between the polar star and the sun. "Accumulating" impulses that surround the stars and planets, it formulates the paternal energies mentioned above (*ilbissin, abyssyn, d'elbissin, chydyrman*) and *aru neme*, which is pure solar matter. The Blue Creator directs these energies in the direction of the earth in the form of spirits; spirits of good and evil, doubt, confirmation, and awareness. Here they are magnetically pulled by the moon's invisible companion, the Blue Embodier through which they pass. As a result, the beginnings of the human soul (*suus*) and other living substances are born.

Suus can be understood as the very first, "heavenly" phase in the development of the human soul awaiting earthly embodiment. The soul's paternal essence contains the positive charge *syulter*, which must unite with the maternal essence *saksun*. It is as a result of this process that the earthly embodiment of the soul takes place and a human being appears on the earth. The paternal *suus* of the whole diversity of earthly living beings lie in the heavens above the earth completing multiple cycles: they wait for their earthly embodiment and again return to the skies when their life's journey is complete.

The White Creator, the creator of corporeality, is situated on the *Kangyi* axis between the sun and the earth and likewise attracts and concentrates cosmic energies susceptible to its influence and from them creates the spirits of nature including the spirit of stones, minerals, water, forests, fire, air, and wind. Directed towards the earth, these spirits are pulled by the moon's second invisible companion, the White Embodier, which transforms them into *ak suus,* spirits of dense substance, white substance with a negative charge *saksun* which they receive from Mother Earth.

In earthly life, the unification of paternal and maternal energies signifies *the embodiment of the heavenly spirit and the spiritualization that is the attribution of soul to earthly substance.* This applies as much to man as to the whole diversity of earthly life and animate nature. In this simplified description of the process of creation lies the incredible harmony of earthly life. The interaction between different types of subtle and dense energies creates Nature, so divine in its beauty and power, and gives *structure to the visible world,* filling it with a wealth of content, from the "lifeless" stone to the human soul.

In the teachings of the Nagual (Miguel Ruis), the correlation between earthly and cosmic life sources are portrayed in the following way:

"The universe is a process of unending reproduction. Every planet is a mother constantly busied with the matter of continuing her kin. She decodes information received from the sun which impels her to create life. Messengers of God or angels then carry this information to earth. The essence of light and angels is one and the same. Mother Earth receives the message of light and clothes the 'soul egg' in human flesh. Therefore the egg contains the angelic light received from the sun.

"In essence we are a reproduction of angels or of sunlight. Every one of us is an angel grown in an egg, that is, in the soul. At the same time we have an outer egg which is filled with spirit and linked to the whole cosmos. We are also the material form of our body. You could say that DNA or the base information of life is condensed light. Mother Earth transforms DNA into all possible types of life forms. Every form of light is differentiated by its own unique vibration. One such vibration of solar light is inherent in man. DNA is an information package in sun light. The earth receives it, modifies, and transforms it." (M.K. Nelson. *Beyond the Fear Barrier.* Sophia, 1999)

The birth and life of man take place under the influence of certain life force energies in which the cosmic and earthly essences unite. Depending on their inner nature and the role they play in the development of life on earth, they may be organic (genetic, biological), inorganic, or mystical.

Genetic energy. *Suus* is the human gene/spirit which has absorbed the entirety of cosmic "light" information. In this sense a person is born in the "image and likeness" of *Kangyi*, the Creator. The soul is one small part of a huge world, a "micro-cosmos" containing universal knowledge and energy. This genetic force determines the order and harmony of all animate nature. In the earthly life a person must fulfill their purpose and pass positive energy onto their descendants. In the end a person determines their own life path and circumstances by heeding the voice of spirit. Biological and social inheritance is a product of spiritual, genetic energy. Therefore depending on the strength of spirit, and to what extent an individual follows their purpose, positive characteristics can either take root to be strengthened in the descendants or fade away, eventually being severed.

Biological energy. Biological energy is formed as a result of the interaction between cosmic energy and the energy of animate nature. This is the case with man and the animal and vegetable kingdoms. A person's life-force, growth and nurture depend on this energy. It is considered that currents of cosmic energy coming to earth from the planets and stars affect the human aura. A person receives nourishment not only from food but also from the sunlight, from natural spring water, fresh air and invisible subtle energies that are also essential to one's health. Often in the Altai mountains you can see a light bluish haze (*ynaar tyudyuzek*) which seems to have formed as the result of the unification of different elements including radiation from the sun, "the breath of the earth and vegetation," moisture and the movement of air currents. Such natural phenomena are very wholesome for the human body and soul and can impart a huge charge of energy. Biological energy is also the informational channel by which man can communicate with the animal and plant kingdoms. Through this energy man can find a common language with plants and animals learning to feel and understand them. This channel is more reliable for preserving a unity between man and nature (it would be more accurate to say "for the preservation of man in nature") than contemporary technological attempts to solve ecological problems.

Inorganic energy - crystal energies, magnetism and electricity. This type of energy arises from the influence of cosmic impulses from mountain rock, minerals and metals and from tiny particles of dispersed matter in *chaiykoma*, atoms, and molecules. It is through inorganic energy that the body and soul are permanently linked to nature and from this source qualities such as durability, firmness, strength and speed are found. The earth is linked to the cosmos by electromagnetic radiation through which cooperation takes place with the sun, stars and other planets. At the current time the influence of technological factors on the earth's magnetic and electrical fields has greatly increased. This not only has a negative effect on the earth's climate and weather but also destroys the electromagnetic carcass of the whole solar system. As a result of the intensive development of new communication systems (satellite and mobile networks) in radio range, the earth "shines" brighter than the sun and radio exchange gets jammed between the sun and other planets (see A.N. Dmitriev, p.47).

Mystical energies and spirits. According to Altai White Believers, light white substances - *ak neme* and *Kangyi* energies rise upwards into the firmament and are incarnated into gods and angels. *Burkhans* are sacred places where the soul is born and develops. According to Altai legend, angels are the sons and daughters of gods. Heavier white substances and energies found on the earth's surface are called *ee* (spirits). Spirits usually take the form of human beings or of a sacred animal. For example, the spirit of Altai (*Altai-kudai*) is said to be a man with a white beard in white clothing on a white horse. His wife (*Umai-ene*) is a woman. The spirit of *arzhan suu* (healing spring) is a girl. The forest spirit *Shangyr* is a man. The spirit of the mountains can show itself in the form of a deer, etc. *Altai-kudai* is sometimes shown as a bright colour and in the form of a square with eight rays which represents the immutability of the laws of life. It may also be indicated on flints in the form of a peony depicted with six or eight petals as an all-encompassing symbol of nature.

The white substance of mystical energy affects a person's fate and determines their everyday life. *Jarlykchi* (clairvoyants who interact with mystical energies) are able to obtain information about forthcoming events or a person's health because the soul of every individual is indivisibly linked to *Kangyi*.

White substance, however, is always opposed by black substance. Black substance lies heavier in *Kangyi* like a sediment and resides in the lower seven layers of Mother Earth. *Kams* (shamans) are the mediators between black substance and human beings, whereas *jarlykchi* act as mediators between man and white substance. Herein lies the harmony of the construction of *Kangyi* and the construction of human life: In *Kangyi* the forces of both good and evil are found, and each of them according to their nature strives to obtain what it requires from every individual soul. Therefore, the purpose of mystical energies lies in the fact that they are a kind of mediator between the subtle world of *Kangyi* and the world of human beings. *Kangyi* embodies good and evil in the human world via the spirits.

Kangyi is indeed one like the endless blue sky above us. It is just that different peoples in different parts of the world refer to it differently: *Kangyi* above *"Kan Altai"* is referred to by the Altai people as *"Altai-Kudai,"* "God Altai." In Europe and the Mediterranean people call *Kangyi*, "Christ"; in Asia, "Allah" and "Buddha." Perhaps, at some point in the future, different nationalities will come to a point of mutual understanding in their conception of the Highest.

Spirituality and the Soul

The soul – states and stages

Traditional notions of the origin, qualities, and development of the soul are relatively complex. The different aspects of the soul, its "structure," conditions, and various phases of development, are well represented, however, in the Altai language. In general it is said that the soul acts as a person's double, providing a connection with the subtle worlds. The double is capable of visiting worlds that the physical body cannot.

Tyn The soul, (in Altai, "*tyn*") is the capacity for life, breath and growth, peculiar not only to man but to the entire natural world. Nothing in nature is inanimate. Water, air and even a single stone breathe and have spirit and so are considered living beings. "*Tash eelu, tash ta tyndu*" means "stone with spirit, the stone is alive." Of humans and animals it is said: "*Tiryu tyn*," which means "living soul, living and breathing." Distinctions are drawn between different types of energy, for example, organic, as in the animal kingdom, or inorganic, as in the case of a stone.

Ozok is the word for the soul's center, located in the cells of the chest area and central to *bilik* concepts of wisdom. *Ozok* is composed of a positive charge (*syulter*) and a negative charge (*saksun*). This composition allows for mergence between the male and the female essence (that which is of heaven and that which is of the earth). The center of the soul (*ozok*) contains the genetic energy that determines a person's heredity, fate, psychological makeup, and level of wisdom. All that is placed in the center of the soul is gradually made manifest through our thoughts and consciousness (*shunu*).

Syulter, the positive charge, is capable of leaving the body during sleep. It can move through space, receive information concerning the past, present, and future, and communicate with heavenly and human spirits, both of the living and the deceased. Most people experience this phenomenon in a dream state, but clairvoyants possessed of particular gifts or with developed abilities can communicate with the subtle worlds consciously and retrieve important information. It is said that *syulter* particularly likes to visit the land of its ancestors and is drawn to the sacred spirit of *tes*.

Saksun, the negative charge, unlike *syulter*, always remains in the body and is considered the body's guardian and protector. In Altai it is forbidden to disturb, let alone excavate, graves because *saksun* may take vengeance not only on those who have

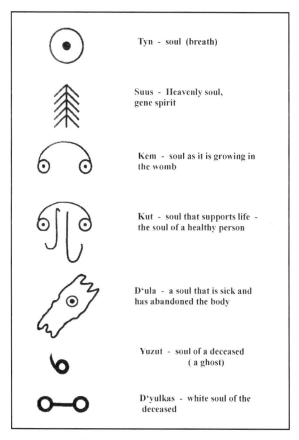

Figure 3. Stages of the soul

disturbed the peace of the deceased but also on anyone living nearby. This is one of the reasons why the Altai people protest so strongly against the actions of archaeologists who have been excavating ancestral burial mounds, *kurgans*, in Altai on a huge scale.

According to beliefs concerning *tyn,* the soul develops cyclically passing through many phases and conditions over the period of a person's life.

Suus The soul of every individual has *suus,* that is, its divine embodiment and it is the joy of each individual that of countless number of souls one's own particular *suus* was chosen and given to the mother's womb to take physical form and develop in the conditions of earthly life. The divine essence of the soul, *suus* (the gene spirit) carries the "genetic" information of *Kangyi,* and its manifestation occurs as a result of the interaction of the various cosmic and earthly energies mentioned above. Once embodied on earth, *suus* not only determines a person's individuality but also governs their connection with the universe, with all the information of *Kangyi,* and the knowledge of invisible worlds.

Jarlykchi can "see" these *suus,* a countless number of which are located in different layers of the sky called *burkhans.* They are linked by invisible threads (*surguld'yn*), which carry information (*aidylga*). This genetic energy is also said to take the form of tiny beads (*suluzunov*).

Suus consists of two parts, male and female. Before entering the womb, *suus* splits into two to be embodied separately entering the womb of two different mothers. There may be a time lapse between one conception and the other, but under normal circumstances, the average quantity of men and women within one age group is approximately the same. If both parts then find each other later in life, the couples' lives together will be happy and harmonious. Of such couples it is said: "they are a match made in heaven." At the moment of conception *suus* takes on its embodiment and the soul of the future individual begins to receive the genetic information carried in *suus* from *Kangyi* that will determine that person's function in life and his or her particular psychological makeup. It would seem that it is impossible to change the information pertaining to destiny and purpose that is imprinted in the womb.

Even the heart's instinctive ability to recognize a person as familiar or unfamiliar, called *syrkyn*, (some people we instinctively warm to while others immediately put us on our guard, depending on the energies of kindness or malice, wisdom or foolishness that radiate from their soul) is present in the center of the soul at the moment of conception.

It is said that a person's fate is determined by *Ene-Dzhaiachi*, the Mother-Creator. If conception takes place at the new moon, with a morning star and in the sunlight when there are a greater number of pure cosmic and earthly energies in *Kangyi*, then a person's fate is set on a path of kindness from the very beginning. Furthermore, if at the moment of conception one receives *chydyrman* (strengthening particles), then one is destined to live longer than the average lifespan *enchi chak* (72 years). Such a person will find an honoured position in life according to their own strengths and abilities and by their own efforts achieve happiness and abundance. Such individuals often become leaders, greatly influencing their environment and working for the development of society.

If conception takes place at the old moon under an evening star when a larger number of darker energies are present in *Kangyi*, then a person's fate is plotted on a darker path. This does not mean that for such a soul, the road to grace is closed, because the inherited energy of *suus* is always white and pure. There will, however, always be an ongoing battle in the soul between the pure *suus* energies and the darker energies absorbed at conception. Which side takes precedence depends greatly upon the circumstances of one's life, but ultimately each individual must determine the quality of their own path. A person may call on their own awareness, belief in the power of goodness, and the wisdom of others for support. On the path of self development, cleansing the soul of dark energies, envy, and malice makes a person significantly stronger. The path to grace may not be direct, but such a person may walk this path more surely than another whose soul has not known such trial and initiation.

As a rule, people who are fated to be superbly kind or particularly malicious are few. Most are changeable in their behavior, receiving fluctuating energies at the soul center. Such people may be kind or malicious depending on circumstances and the influence of others. They too must make their choices in life and may also achieve success and prosperity. Their place in society and position will be determined by their inherited ability to adapt, to attune to, and to accommodate dark or light energies.

Having said that one's fate and purpose (*salym*) is placed at the center of the soul at the moment of conception. Responsibility lies with the individual to manifest this potential. The realization of one's fate depends on the peculiarities of one's psyche and temperament. These qualities are also placed in the soul at the moment of conception according to the influence of cosmic energies. This information is contained in one's ancestral *suus*. Whether a person will be happy-go-lucky and dynamic, passive and melancholy, or fluctuate between the two depends also on the condition of their psychic energy.

Kem While in the womb, the soul is referred to as *kem*. It is the responsibility of the parents to look after the soul of their child at this stage so that it should not be lost. In Altai the artificial abortion of *kem* is hugely taboo.

At birth a child acquires various energies from *Kangyi*, present in the immediate environment. These might be energies of clean substance (*aru neme*), white substance (*ak neme*), fluctuating yellow substance (*berklik neme, sary neme*), or even dark substance (*kara neme*). Such energies are received from the child's parents, midwife or godmother, and anyone else present at birth. The influence of these energies on a person's soul depends on the sun, stars (the morning or evening star), the lunar cycle (new moon, full moon, and old moon), and the year, etc.

Together, these energies form an aura (*kurchuu*) around the body of the newborn. The aura then unites with the center of the soul (*tyn*) with a great number of invisible strands (*surguldyn*) at which point the child gives its first cry! The aura protects the soul and the body from negative influences in the environment.

All these different conditions and circumstances go together to form the aura and define one's temperament, peculiarities of behavior, psychological makeup, and other differentiating personal qualities. In contrast to the direction of one's fate and temperament, a person's character can change according to lifestyle, environment, and upbringing. Every new phase in a person's life demands changes of some kind or another and involves correcting one's personality in certain ways. It is, for example, customary to make the following blessing to those newly wed, embarking on the journey of marriage: one asks that the husband be *tenzhe*, which means "level and calm," and that the wife be *shinirleler*, which means "malleable, able to attune to and adapt to her husband."

Over the period of one's life, the aura of one's soul becomes tired, weaker, and gradually consumed by dark substances. A person may periodically strengthen the aura by carrying out prayers in sacred mountains or even on the plains of steppe areas in energetically clean and powerful places. Churches, mosques, and temples were earlier built in such places.

Kut The healthy soul of an adult is called *kut*. This is the force that supports life. The health of one's body and soul, one's life force, depends on the quality of the connection between *syulter* and *saksun* at the center of the soul. (*Syulter* and *saksun* are connected by an "arch of light," a radiance called *surguld'yn*.) It is sometimes the case that a person strong in spirit is weak in health although strength of spirit can also overcome illness and physical weakness. There are those who have been known to recklessly waste a warrior's health. One manifestation of heredity (the genetic energy of *Kangyi*, including the memory of the ancestors) is that a person who has received a large quantity of strengthening energy in their aura at birth achieves great strength of will and longevity. A man with a weak spirit whose paternal energies are weak at the soul center is unable to provide strong support for a woman. This can be the result of heredity, as the souls of the ancestors returning to *Kangyi* carry their own energy with them, be they weak or strong. *Saksun* that accumulates in the body of Mother Earth can have a positive or negative effect.

D'yula. *Jarlykchi* say that if a person has been seriously ill, then their *kut* leaves the body and becomes *dyula,* a sickly soul. It is the responsibility of the *jarlykchi* to find the lost soul and return it to the body, after which the individual should recover.

Yyuzut. If the threads between *syulter* and *saksun* in the soul center are broken a person dies. On the threshold of death the soul becomes *yyuzut*. *Yyuzut* can be white or black depending on the deeds of one's earthly life. On the fortieth day after death the *yyuzut* is judged and its future path determined. It is said that as a test the *yyuzut* must sit on a blade of grass. If the person is light and pure, then the blade will not bend. In this case the soul is referred to as *d'yulkas*, the "white soul of the deceased." Such souls become the white spirits of the homeland (*ak tester*). They remain on the earth to unite with *Kangyi*. They return to *suus* and await their next earthly incarnation. The Altai people do not have a concept of heavenly paradise. It is for the individual to make their happiness here in the earthly life.

If a person has committed actions that have significantly destroyed the balance of harmony in the external world their *yyuzut* will become dark, black and heavy and the stalk will bend. In such cases, whether or not the individual was aware of the consequences of their actions is of no account. Either way, the actions will be reflected in the *yyuzut*. It is for this reason that our ancestors took great care and had great concern for moral purity and spiritual upbringing.

The evaluation of *yyuzut* is based on six conditions:

1 The reason for the action - kindness or malice
2 The result of the action
3 The possible justification before God for any harm caused
4 The motivation for the action - white or black
5 The individual's condition on committing the action
6 The individual's spiritual awareness, broad or narrow, light or dark

The soul with a dark *yyuzut* goes to *tamy (tamug)* - "hell," and is called *syune*, the "black soul of the deceased." It remains in *tamy* until it has become cleansed through suffering. Once cleansed it returns to *Kangyi* to become *suus* and again embody the earthly life.

It is said that *suus* can also "wear out" and "die," and that *syune*, dark souls on occasion permeate into *Kangyi*. *Kangyi* in turn cleanses itself of them with thunder and lightning. Weak, impure *suus* is "buried" in the earth by storms. According to folk lore, a tree struck by lightning should be avoided and it is forbidden to use such trees for specific purposes, such as firewood or building materials, as they are considered to be the graves of heavenly *suus*. In recent years, both scientists and the local population have noted changes in the frequency and form of lightning and electric storms in Altai. It is said that lightning has come "alive."

When dark souls of the deceased accumulate in large quantities they cause Mother Earth to suffer like an infected wound. "Cosmic healers" such as the Blue Creator, White Creator, the sun, and others come to her assistance. As a result, natural catastrophes, floods, earthquakes, fires, and other natural disasters, take place under the influence of cosmic impulses. Nature cleanses itself and so people who consider themselves sensible and aware must consider whether they are living in the correct way on earth, and whether their actions are for the good. The ideas within the *bilik* about the fiery, cosmic cleansing of the Earth coincide surprisingly with contemporary, scientific conclusions set forth in the studies of Professor A.N. Dmitriev, "Fiery recreation of the Earth's climate." It is believed that the time will come when *Kangyi* will cleanse itself fully of dark substances with fire, after which the "white" age of justice will dawn.

Ethics – the heart, chest and liver

It has already been said that everything that is placed in the center of the soul gradually becomes manifest in one's consciousness (*shyunyu*). Through its divine essence, the soul is connected to *Kangyi*, which can be described as an energetic-information system. The soul is nourished with heavenly light and cosmic energies. In its turn the soul radiates psychic energies, be they of grace or evil, peace or tension, love and cooperation or aggression. This exchange of energies and infor-mation between the soul and *Kangyi,* of which the soul is a tiny part, normally takes place unconsciously on the part of the individual *shyunyut* (the subconscious).

However, the very same energies within *Kangyi* that are focused by the soul center do influence a person's consciousness, using the brain as an instrument. It is thanks to these energies that human thought can be so strong, powerful, and all pervasive. Human thought is capable of penetrating to the very essence of things, instantaneously traversing huge distances in time and space. *Human thought, born in a condition of love and harmony with the world, Nature, and fellow man, united with one's own will can create miracles and truly change the world.*

According to the *bilik*, thought, *(sanal)* is the action of psychic energy, developed by the brain and radiated in the form of waves (sounds, impulses), which reflect the external world, taking shape in thoughts and words.

A thought can be sent over huge distances. In one's thoughts one may turn to the spirit of one's homeland, to one's mother and to other loved ones. *The power of one's thought is dictated by the soul's center and by strength of spirit.* Thought also depends on the physical and emotional condition of a person at any given time. A thought wave sent in a moment of fear can be felt by the soul of a mother, father, or child, even at great distance.

Thought energy can penetrate to the depths and secrets of a person's consciousness and there find lost or hidden information. With thought one may restore that which has been lost and differentiate between truth and deception. Far from every individual is possessed of such power. Human consciousness and thought derive their power through their connection with *tyn,* the soul centre. Just as the soul, being a tiny part of *Kangyi,* contains its energetic-informational strength, so is the quality of consciousness analogical to the quality of *Kangyi.* Human consciousness and thought derive their energy from this source. The difference between one individual and another is simply in the scale and power of their thoughts. *Kangyi* is immense and unbounded, whereas every individual has limits to their capability for thought and depth of consciousness.

The unification of *syulter* and *saksun* in the soul center animates the body and fuels the consciousness. It defines one's fate along a light, dark, or winding path. A person's behavior also greatly depends on the impact of cosmic particles and invisible rays from Earth-Mother at conception and at birth. The ability for independent thought is therefore essential in the process of one's personal development. Only when one has learned independent thought can one unite the heart with reason, the consciousness with the sub-conscious and, on this basis, embody clear thought in action. It is only in hindsight that the majority of people can perceive where they have erred in their thoughts or feelings. That is why it is said, "Everyone makes mistakes."

In some people thought energy manifests quickly, even immediately, while in others it manifests slowly or hardly has any impact at all. This depends in part on the genetic energy of the soul, *kut*. A person can intellectually analyze all their actions and correct their mistakes, but thoughts are sent by the soul center from the chest cells. This is why it is said: "trust your heart," "your heart will know," for it is in the chest cells at the center of the soul that human wisdom abides.

Altai people believe that a more dependable answer to a question or solution to a problem comes not from the head, but from the chest cells, *kegyus* (this word contains three meanings: "chest," "heart," and "wisdom"). In Altai it is said, "*kegyustyu kizhi*," which means "wise person." A wise person enjoys a higher status than *sanaalu kizhi*, a clever person, because consciousness, thought, and desire come initially from the heart, the soul center, rather than from the mind. In a kind, conscientious person the center of the soul is more powerful than the mind.

The *bilik* contains an interesting notion of *kegyus-chakyr*, which refers to the "emptiness" beneath the heart (the heart chakra) which is the "space" where thoughts and feelings are weighed up, enabling a person to find a balanced solution or come to a wise decision. When one is advised to act according to one's conscience, one immediately directs one's attention to the chest area. From then on it depends on one's level of wisdom whether what is evoked there can be applied to one's actions. If a person's actions lack wisdom, it is said, "the empty part in your heart doesn't work."

The same notion of "emptiness" is linked with the work of awareness and intellect that takes place in the upper part of the head, the chakra, connecting a person to cosmic mind. When a person is incapable of thinking reasonably, it is said, "the emptiness in your head doesn't work." The liver is the "spiritual organ" that determines a person's ability to feel subtle energies and sense other people. Researchers of Altai beliefs and moral teachings have noted correctly that the Altai faith is marked by an absence of religious moral system. In the *bilik*, the fate and purpose of an individual is determined by *Ene-dzhaiachi* (Mother-Creator). Therefore, a person must accept with dignity that which has been dealt him by the heavens. This is the luggage with which one comes into the world. However, one's behaviour and actions in various life situations, choosing good or evil, depends totally on the individual. Of course, one depends on the qualities received at birth, such as one's disposition, personality traits and unconscious knowledge. It depends on the individual alone whether during their lifetime they can improve and augment what has been given them by the heavens. Therefore, development of the soul is given high priority in a person's life.

Rather than adopting a specific moral teaching, it is thought that blessings and good wishes spoken in solemn tones can be more helpful at significant moments in a person's life. It is said that blessings are helpful to a person's spiritual development, supportive of their striving towards the good and can be effective in positively influencing a person's behavior.

Good wishes (*alkysh*) made in poetic form are ubiquitous in the Altai language. Blessings are made at weddings and the celebration of a birth or significant birthday (according to the six year calendar system). In Altai folk tradition there are also many prohibitions. It is considered taboo, for example, to climb to the very peak of a sacred mountain. This particularly refers to young women. It is forbidden to shout or make loud noises in sacred places, to pour dirty water into a river or to call a respected person by their first name instead of *aky* (honourable), etc. Such prohibitions are based on generations of life experience and have been incorporated into ancient customs and traditions.

According to the *bilik,* the rejuvenation of the aura may be assured by means of prayer held in sacred mountains on special days such as *d'azhyl byur* (green leaves) at the beginning of summer (the same day as the Trinity in ancient Russian pagan times) and *sary byur* (yellow leaves) in autumn. Over the period of one's life, black substances permeate the soul and can cause psychological illness. A *jarlykchi* can cleanse a human soul of black energies using the ritual *alas* (cleansing the aura with fire or smudging with smoke from a juniper branch, and saying blessings). They believe that the fire of mountain juniper burns away black substance and dark energy and strengthens the soul.

We have not yet learned however, how to truly educate, let alone cleanse, the human soul. That the soul may be cleansed by *tes,* the spirit of the homeland, pride in one's family, and the spirits of the ancestors has long since been forgotten. It is interesting to note that in the past, public birching was carried out not to cause pain and frighten the accused but rather to cleanse the soul. With cries of pain from *kegyus* (the chest cells), dark substance abandoned the body and the soul was cleansed. This procedure was carried out only with the agreement of the accused and only with a clear understanding of the purpose of the procedure to cleanse the soul of the dark substance that incited the individual to commit their crime.

Traditional soul cleansing is also based on the view that an indissoluble link exists between the human soul and *Kangyi.* On the one hand the soul is created by the energies of *Kangyi.* On the other hand *Kangyi* permanently surrounds one and is constantly interacting with and absorbing the energy of living souls.

Raising one's awareness and widening one's consciousness is another way of educating and cleansing the soul. Hence there is so much emphasis in the *bilik* on the practice of self development and the teaching of spirituality. If, for example, a person who has committed a foolish crime is ready to confess and swear never to commit such a crime again, such a person would at the same time acknowledge that they had violated the laws of *Altai-Kudai*, the god of Nature in Altai. They would acknowledge the presence of *kegyus*, the wisdom in the chest cells, and the feelings of the liver.

A person who has violated these precepts may display three shortcomings. Of some it is said, *"kegyus d'ok, kegyuske ilinbegen,"* which means they have no wisdom. It is also said: *"kuru kegyus"* (meaning "empty wisdom,") or *"chalang bash"* (meaning "distracted head"), indicating that although a person sees, hears and feels what is happening in the world around them, their perception, logic and ability to make things conscious remain undeveloped. Such a person may hope to do good, but acts superficially and so the opposite result is achieved.

Of another, it may be said that they are *d'yrtyk bashtu* (a forgetful person). Such a person is not the master of their own words and actions and lives mechanically, often committing actions they later regret.

The third forgets deliberately. Of such a person, it is said, *"byrttu bashtu,"* (a head with black matter, a bad person). The soul and consciousness of a person like this are said to be filled with dark substance. Such people are few, but they exist nonetheless and can cause much harm. Although they may have received good instruction and admonition, and received direction a hundred times, this type of person is unlikely to create goodness until such time as life itself forces them to change.

How can a person rid themselves of such shortcomings if they should discover them in their soul? The *bilik* holds that above all, the desire for good is required, the desire to work against evil and to be more honest with oneself. The desire for self development is required in order to nobly bring up one's own children. The first step towards action is to acknowledge that there is a kind of sickness in one's soul that projects one towards the darkness, creating fear and overstepping moral norms.

When considering issues such as the norms and criteria of

morality one requires a standard or measure. According to the *bilik* this measure is *Altai-Kudai*, the spirit of nature; *tes*, the spirit of the homeland. The natural world of one's homeland offers a perfect example of harmony and the interaction of different forms of life, where the existence and development of one life form provides the conditions for the existence and development of another. It is Nature that teaches man the laws of life and death, the laws of righteousness and the measure of good and evil. Man strives to live within these laws so as not to destroy the harmony of life.

One's conscience, the voice of the soul and the heart, is the regulator for adhering to moral norms common to all men, irrespective of religion, origin, nationality or social position. No one wishes to be called dishonest, unscrupulous, or to be thought badly of, which only causes one's family and children to suffer. No one wishes for their soul to be found darkened after death, or to think that they will be remembered unkindly by others. The conscience reminds one to consider the purity of one's soul and whether it has become darkened from unkind acts or by allowing envy, vengeance, slander, arrogance, or greed into one's heart. These characteristics are the root of all evil but can be corrected through the desire for spiritual purity.

The acknowledgment of one or another of these shortcomings in oneself is the first step towards purifying one's soul. If a person acknowledges their mistakes and shortcomings superficially, but without a deeper sense of conviction there can be no healing. One's thoughts must first pass through *kegyus*, the center of the soul, the heart and the liver. Unless there is a sense of conviction and sincerity, heavy, black sediment will build up in the soul. If one's awareness has passed through *kegyus*, then there will be cleansing. This is the beginning of healing; the second step is to initiate recovery.

The next step in the path to healing can also be achieved with the help of a *jarlykchi*, his blessing and ritual. In this case, a *jarlykchi* helps the human soul to unite with *Altai-Kudai*, the spirit of Nature. The acknowledgment of the words of a *jarlykchi* and through him of *Altai-Kudai* is what is referred to as spiritual medicine. The laws of Nature are sacred and so, in accepting them and assimilating them with conviction, a person takes further steps on the path towards healing.

There are cases in which a person has not directly caused harm themselves but nonetheless, their soul knows no rest. Given the understanding of the bilik, in cases such as these one should consider what harm may have been caused by a parent or relative. In one's own life one must consider one's children, as repentance and acknowledgment of negative acts and 'mistakes' can be released through the body and soul of one's offspring causing them to suffer.

It is said that no one can be totally pure, but that there are many who work for the good. After death the *syulter* of people like these unite with the spirit of the homeland and continue to help people in earthly matters before they leave for the sky to become *suus* (the gene spirit) again.

Love and harmony

It is natural to experience feelings of love and kindness towards those we are close to, such as a mother, father, or friend. These feelings may also extend to the work we are passionate about or to one's homeland. However, without consciously engaging in the inner work of the soul, even the strongest feelings can fade with time. Love and desire are not evoked by the negative or unkind. That which is negative however, can evoke interest and develop dependency. Without cleansing the consciousness, harmful or foolish desires and inclinations can become consolidated.

Various desires in the form of impulses constantly circulate between the consciousness and the heart, and desires that often repeat themselves become permanent feelings, consistent emotions. It is wise therefore to consciously choose which desires, emotions and thoughts one wishes to strengthen and which one sees fit to discard. That which is strengthened remains in the subconscious.

Any kind, rational feeling experienced subconsciously in one's youth, when a person is beginning to establish themselves as an independent being, goes towards forming their view of the world later in life. When impulses, desires, and feelings have passed many times between the consciousness of the brain, the wisdom of the heart, and the sensitivity of the liver, they have completed the impulse cycle in the human soul. These impulses strive to repeat the path of the cycle and so in the case of positive feelings a feeling of love can develop. It is said that in the years after the age of thirty-six these impulses become brighter, cleansing themselves of harmful matter and dark energies.

In the process of circulation, the impulses of the soul become brighter and firmer and, as such, love receives *alkyn* (a firm place in the soul). This resolution is cultivated firstly in one's consciousness, then passes through the center of the soul and the heart and takes root there. This process provides a person with lifelong happiness and a sense of fulfillment. A person who has strengthened their soul through self development and spiritual teaching eventually has no need of advice, direction or moral instruction. Their fate, psyche and temperament stand fast, creating a firm foundation on the path of life.

If a person wishes to be loved they must first of all love themselves as an integral part of *Kangyi*. For a religious person this means to love oneself as a part of the one God. Love for oneself does not include conceited self interest. To love oneself, a person must develop their best qualities through the genuine desire to be pure and light according to their own will. To love oneself one must experience the personal desire to take care of the solar and light energies received from *Kangyi* and from

Mother-Earth, and try to develop these in one's physical body and soul. After the age of thirty-six one may begin to pass this experience of cultivating one's feelings on to one's children, grandchildren, and great grandchildren through the hereditary tradition of pride, family name and honour. This reflects the algorithms of life. Only through the combination of the positive and the negative can a person discover how to purify their feelings and desires.

One wonders why is seems so difficult to teach what is good and positive, whilst evil seems to demand no real teaching at all. Today the harmony of life appears to manifest in such curious forms. An elderly person might refer to one of the creation myths and say that this is because *Erlik* tricked *Ulgen* and so man was given his soul by *Erlik*. This slant on the creation myth probably appeared in the "black era," the era of darkness. They say that after the creation of man, *Ulgen* and *Erlik* made an agreement. *Ulgen* would record man's good deeds on his palms and *Erlik* would record man's evil deeds on his. Whereas man's good deeds all fitted onto one of *Ulgen's* palms, *Erlik* wrote man's evil deeds on his palms and then all over his body and in this way became "darkened." In life, the manifestation of evil deeds depends on the action of *abisinov* (energies of evil that saturate *Kangyi*). According to the *bilik*, the "white age" has not yet begun. We are still at the end of the "yellow age" when black substances (*kara neme*) preside over white substances (*ak name*). This is a time of preparation for a change in epoch (*enchelik*).

At this time of transition, most people's actions are subject to the influence of dark substance. The ability to be wise is largely suppressed and consciousness is cloaked with "viruses" of evil. Almost every individual thinks only of how he might earn money. Over time, many have become used to "evil," and so suffering and injustice have become quite normal phenomena in their lives. People have lost much of their ability to discern good (*tuza*) from evil (*tyubek*). The difference has been eroded from mass consciousness.

In this lies one of the peculiarities of the overall condition of harmony in our time. One's own reason is no longer always adequate in discerning issues of morality. In Russia there is the proverb: "Their intentions were good, but things turned out as they always do." Today, happiness and goodness seem inaccessible to many, whereas in actual fact they are just "in the dark," in a place of no clarity *(bilderbes)*, and this can have a deciding influence over people's actions.

It is very difficult under such conditions to teach what is good and positive while life itself teaches what is negative. White Believers consider this to be a temporary condition rather than the eternal "wheel" of human suffering. We know that happiness and suffering replace one another in a person's life. Herein lies another peculiarity of the harmony of our time. We ask ourselves whether what is happening is for better or for worse. This is determined by today's harmony. Every searching individual must answer this question for themselves and each will answer it differently.

The White Faith aims only to give guidance. The guidance offered consists of four aspects, which conclude in an understanding of how one might move beyond a condition of *bilderbes*, the position of no clarity. This guidance *(alad'ak)* is aimed at teaching harmony in the life of man according to nature's laws. This is referred to as *ala*, harmony.

Firstly, it is held that one must determine one's true purpose in life *(d'yuryumnin amaduzyn)*. For most people the purpose of life consists in getting up, washing, eating, going to work, returning home, eating again, resting, watching television, reading, doing something about the home, and then going to bed. That said, man differs from other earthly beings in clarity of mind, depth of soul, and understanding of the meaningfulness of life. To overcome a condition of negativity and unhappiness it is essential that one strives towards the fulfillment of one's own life purpose. This might involve taking account of one's abilities and current resources and doing something good for those close to you or those in need, or something for the common good of society. The most important thing is that one's actions leave one with a sense of goodness and that one's conscience be satisfied. It is feeling rather than purely rational thought that must dictate one's actions.

Secondly, one must constantly support the inner desire to continue revealing more about one's life purpose, step by step overcoming obstacles, displaying strong will power, constantly searching for that which is new, and recreating one's life for the better.

Thirdly, to fulfill the second direction, one must constantly search for strong moral and spiritual guidance (*alkyn*), and develop principles (*alad'ak*) in practical matters. This might include intentions such as acknowledging and correcting one's mistakes, helping other people, being less dependent on stimulants, visiting one's parents, making time to talk to children, etc. *Alkyn* (guidance) is developed over a long period of time within oneself whereas *alad'ak* (principles) are developed through concrete action.

Fourthly, to develop good instruction in one's daily life it is essential to develop "long will" (*chydun*), and to enlighten one's mind with wisdom (oi). It is important to raise one's awareness of how to act with justice and overcome discord and disagreement among others. One should strive to learn how to refine one's personal goal and remain focused on that goal for the good of all. *Ala* (harmony) is contained within the idea of defining one's purpose and discovering the significance of human life. It involves developing a belief in the continuation of the human race. It presupposes striving towards happiness and the awareness that those are happy who create goodness in their own lives and the lives of others.

The wisdom that enables a person to achieve *ala* (harmony) in their behavior and actions develops over three stages:

The first stage involves comprehending cause and effect in events on the basis of rational thinking. The second stage involves accepting the results of the thinking in one's soul center (*kegyus*), which implies an awareness of harmony achieved through the unification of the heart and mind. The third stage involves creating links with the subtle worlds and the spirit of Nature, (mystical energies), with the help of White Faith rituals that enable a person to observe the laws and rules of the subtle world. The spirits of Nature enable a person to gain a true sense of harmony and morality, and discern where good and evil lie.

Through communication with the subtle worlds a person comes to understand what creates happiness and what creates suffering in the real world. Happiness is created through "white substance." The light energy of *Kangyi* comes through the white spirits. If a person worships white energy only, avoiding all dark spirits, then he has accepted the White Faith. Coming into contact with mystical energy, one comes to understand that suffering (*shyra*) is caused by "dark substances" present in *Kangyi*, that is, by "dark spirits." Suffering may be caused by dark thoughts, curses, and envy of others. In practical life, dark energies are referred to as dark viruses (*byrt abyssyny*).

Communicating with the subtle world, a person attunes themselves to the harmony of life, and so discovers happiness. The conception of happiness is, of course, relative, as an individual's sense of happiness depends on their fate, psychological make-up and temperament, irrespective of social position, creed, education, etc. Generally, a person is happy who has succeeded in developing the purest qualities (*kylyk*) of their soul. *Kylyk sanaa eechir* means, "character follows thought and vision." The well being of one's family, success at work, one's disposition, etc., all depend on the purity of one's striving.

In the White Faith, there are no moral dictates like those in Christianity: "Thou shalt not kill, thou shalt not steal," etc. In one's self-development one draws on blessings (*alkysh*), guidance (*alkyn*), and directions (*aladak*). White Faith infers great freedom and independence on the individual, perhaps more so than in other religions. However, this independence is accepted as existing within the context of certain limits of responsibility before Mother Nature. This is ultimately considered to be for the benefit of humanity in future cycles in the one great cycle of life.

The notion of *ala* (harmony) also defies the existence of a barrier between material and spiritual culture. Science generally assumes that the material dimension of life determines a man's thinking. Buddhism, on the other hand, teaches that a person's consciousness determines their earthly, material life. According to the Altai faith, nothing in the middle world is without physical manifestation. Consciousness is physical made up of the invisible white substance (aru name) and the energy of *Kangyi*. The *bilik* affirms that the subtle world (*ol d'er*), consists of *ak neme* (white substance), *kara neme* (black substance), and *aru neme* (pure substance). The spiritual culture of every individual is an integral part of *Kangyi*, a very real part of the subtle world.

It is worth mentioning one more characteristic of *ala* (harmony) in contemporary life. Discord arises in today's society most often due to differences in life style. A person who is very rich may work no harder than one who is poor. The poor may become resentful of the wealthy, particularly if they are in a position of authority, be it as civil servant or boss. The *bilik* is not a proponent of material equality, but *ala* (harmony) includes the understanding of a measured life style in which each individual meets their essential needs. It is considered only natural that each individual be clothed, fed and have a roof over their heads with a little extra resources which enable one to help others, particularly one's children, who may not yet have reached a position of independence. This is considered a norm.

In the past, the expression *'byiandu bai'* was used in reference to a person who shared his abundance with others. The expression *'ankan d'ydu bai'* referred to a selfish, greedy person and has connotations of stench. Of course, no one wished to be branded with such a term and so one did not see the sharp class differentiation that exists in today's society.

Cycles

Cycles 'yuie' in the life of man

In the *bilik*, both one and six are sacred numbers. One Altai legend has it that the God *Ulgen* created life on earth in six days. The number six is a particularly significant number in the counting of natural cycles. To this day, the base of the *ail* (traditional Altai dwelling) is built in the shape of a hexagon. The wooden tethering post which stands just outside each ail is marked with six notches which symbolize the six cycles *'yuie'* in a person's life.

According to Altai belief, the soul develops cyclically and, as has already been mentioned in previous chapters, passes through six different stages of development over the course of a lifetime: heavenly *suus, kem, kut, d'yula, yyuzut* and *d'yulkas* or *syune*. These cycles are closely related to another six phases of chronological and physical development called *yuie*. These phases begin at birth and continue up to the predetermined time of one's death.

Nowadays, it is customary to celebrate one's birthday every year, holding particularly large celebrations at significant ages. However, in former times it was custom to celebrate one's birthday only once every twelve years when one reached y*uie*, a significant stage within the six-year counting system. At these times in a person's life one would receive blessings from close relatives (*alkysh*), and attune one's consciousness (*shyunyut*), projecting it forward towards the next twelve-year period in one's life with the aim of living well. In doing this, one's consciousness begins to prepare for the next stage of initiation and learning in one's life, keeping one's conscience clear before the memory of one's ancestors.

The six stages *yuie* are as follows:

First yuie: Childhood. A pair of child "years" (6+6=12years).

At the age of twelve it is considered that an individual has reached the age of youth. Over childhood one subconsciously assimilates the ancestral and parental way of life. Then, the time comes to prepare the young soul for family life. With this aim a betrothal (*kadak*) was traditionally organized. Girls had their hair dressed in one long plait (*ked'ege*) that hung down their back, decorated with the *shanky* adornment, which signified "being accounted for" and the requirement to preserve chastity and honour (*eeren*). Boys also had their hair dressed in a plait at the crown. The responsibility of protecting and guarding two souls, his own and that of his future bride, was impressed upon the boy. Usually, guests were invited for a meal who would express various good wishes, all of which enforced a sense of moral responsibility upon the young individual.

Second yuie: Age of youth (12+12=24 years).

It is supposed that at this age the two 'halves' have already begun creating a family and the young man has moved away from his parents, creating his own home somewhere else, thereby affirming his independence. New values and goals strengthen in the consciousness of the young couple as they bring up their children and further themselves in their work.

Third yuie: Age of independence (12x3=36 years).

The family takes root (*tuutalangan*). The individual strengthens both physically and spiritually, preparing to care for the grandchildren and considering their plans and intentions in relation to the dignity and honour of the family. The knowledge gained from personal experience in the areas of family, work, relationships, and the environment take root in the chest, becoming strong convictions that are made manifest in one's character and actions.

Fourth yuie: Age of maturity (12x4=48 years).

Having acquired experience and strong character, an individual is now able to deal with family and other domestic affairs. Moral consistency and spiritual values should have been strengthened, and clarity achieved in defining values in various spheres of one's life.

Fifth yuie: Age of wisdom (12x5=60 years).

At this stage, the individual begins to draw conclusions about their life and the results of their work, analyzing their successes and failures. Having earned authority and respect, a person now finds themselves able to solve more complex problems and give advice and direction. Consequently people may come to this individual for advice. The individual begins the process of preparing for old age, cleansing the soul before its return to the skies.

Sixth yuie: Predetermined period *enchi chak* (12x6=72 years).

Seventy-two years is considered the average life span. However, those who have received a large number of blessings or much gratitude throughout their lives, or those who are possessed of a special gift and cosmic energy (*chydyrman*) may live longer. Such an individual is venerated and addressed as *aky, d'aanak*, revered, white beard, or grandmother. Such a person achieves the level of moral purity required for the soul to be clean and white when it returns to *Kangyi*.

Cycles of a nation

Altai wise men used the number 72 in other counting systems relevant to clans, families, and the nation as a whole. According to Altai *jarlykchi* (clairvoyants), shifts in the development cycles of individuals and nations are regulated by *Ene-Dzhaiachi*, referred to by Russian pagans of previous centuries as the "Mother-Creator." A *jarlykchi* is usually capable of perceiving the appropriateness of the fate and destiny of an individual and nation through meditation. Over time, experience and knowledge accumulates as folk wisdom such as the laws of natural cycles. The various periods applicable to the cycles of a nation are thought to be as follows:

A nation's youth – up to 72 years.

During the period of a nation's youth individual clans *(sook)* unite and form a single spiritual foundation. During this time an indigenous, national consciousness is formed.

Age of independence – up to 44 years.

During this period a nation strives for independence and autonomy and strengthens its position among other nations. It is at this stage that the mass consciousness is formed.

Age of consolidation – up to 216 years.

The period of consolidation is referred to as *tuutalanar*. The nation begins to recognize the land of its ancestors as national heritage. The basis of the nation's world view and the main branches of its history come together. The nation becomes more profoundly aware of its position among other nations and of its historical mission or purpose.

Age of maturity – up to 288 years.

The process of deeply taking root of a homeland depends both upon the contemporary culture and the history of one's ancestors. Science, national culture, ideology and national consciousness grow from the foundation of myth and legend *(syuldye)*. This is the period in which the accumulated potential of national consciousness is realized.

Age of change and historical choice – up to 360 years.

It was held that during this period a nation reviewed its fate and role in history. The nation's future development or fall has to be considered and depends on the events of the past. If the path has been frustrated with error, weakness and defeat, further development is blocked, whereas if positive potential has been accumulated the nation may evolve further. This is a period which involves interpreting the results of the nation's historical activity based on indigenous national consciousness.

Turning point – up to 432 years.

This stage is called *elen chak,* the allotted period of a nation or clan's activity in the historical arena. The fate of its future existence is decided. A nation may disappear, become scattered, absorbed into a different ethnic group, or take the lead among a larger ethnic group. On the basis of the appraisal of achievements and failures, preparation takes place for transition within national consciousness to a new level of development. If during a certain period the nation has not righted mistakes committed in the past, achieved harmonious social development, or overcome weakness, injustice, and discord, then the nation enters a period of crisis and the future development of its people reaches a deadlock. If during the period of *elen chak* a nation is unable to harmonize its worldview it will begin to die out.

If the historical period has been positive, then another seventy two years is added to the vitality and viability of the nation, achieving a total 504 years (72x7=504). After this period, however, the nation as a whole begins to age. If a nation wishes to prolong its fate it is required to change its worldview in relation to those to whom injustice, offense, or oppression has been caused (such as groups within the nation or other nations). For this to happen, national consciousness must turn to its roots and consider the beginnings of the people's historical development, the formation of the people, its laws and state. The nation must consider its position and history from the point of view of its spiritual source and roots. If this reassessment does not take place then the people will disappear from the historical arena.

Thoughts on cycles in the history of Russia

It is interesting to note that similar stages can be clearly traced in the history of Russia and the Russian people.

The taking of Kazan and the defeat of the Kazan khanate (1552-1555) signified the end of longstanding civil war and the beginnings of the formation of the great Russian nation as successor to the Turkic super-ethnos and Slavic peoples. At this time, a new common Russian state was being created based on the fragments of the obsolete "horde" and "principalities." This turning point inevitably took the form of conflict as the Turkic heritage was disclaimed and reappraised. Gradually, a new mass consciousness and leading ideology emerged.

In the interests of the victorious dynasty official history was rewritten; one religion was replaced by another and peoples, towns, and villages were renamed. Over the natural, historical process of the formation of the Russian state much was inherited from the culture and state of the "horde," although not without deep grievance and oppression among the many peoples who came to be a part of the new Russian state.

From the point of view of the *bilik* notion of cycles it is also interesting to note that 432 years passed between the significant historical dates of 1555 and 1987; 432 years being considered an essential turning point in the fate of a nation.

Perestroika was the term given to describe the process of rethinking the fate and ideology of the Russian nation. It would appear that the spirit of Russia is now going through a period of initiation in which its strength, durability and flexibility is being tested.

An interpretation of contemporary events based on the *bilik* would have it that Russia is undergoing a decisive period in history. If Russian mass consciousness and state policy develops, acting on behalf of all the national subjects and peoples of Russia then the Russian nation will stand its ground. God willing, that will be the case! At that point, according to the Altai belief system, another 72 years will be added to the current history of the Russian state as we know it. According to the *bilik* from then on the Russian worldview will begin to change of its own accord based on cyclical laws of social development because at that time, the Russian nation will have reached the grand age of 504 years!

It may be that this system of cycles explains why a nation

sometimes appears to experience a sudden pull to its historical essence and spiritual roots when it is in the process of forming a new mass consciousness. Just as a tree cannot live without its roots, so a nation degenerates if it fails to renew itself and re-experience the quintessential spirit of the nation. It is no great surprise therefore, that Russia and the territories of the former USSR are marked by mass population movement. Individuals are returning to their roots, to the *tes* (spirit) of the homeland to once again acquire the vitality needed to greet the new era. It is evident, that for many Turkic peoples of Russia, the present time is that "age" when it is essential to return to one's roots and original spiritual source. It is a time when many individuals experience a sense of responsibility for the fate of the nation as a whole. Such is the case in Altai.

Thoughts on cycles in the history of Altai

As far as the history of the Altai nation is concerned, in approximately 1587, the Altai clans (*sook*) united against Mongolian supremacy and refused to pay tribute (*kalan*). Their own khan was appointed, Khan Yoskus-Uul, from the Irkit clan and a military force was formed. On Mount Babirgan not far from the present Altai village of Maima on the left bank of the Katun[15] River, they routed the Mongolian troops under the leadership of Er-Chadak. Soon afterward however, Khan Yoskus-Uul was killed by the Mongolians near the present village of Besh-Ezek. Altai lost its independence in 1756, 169 years after the events of 1587, when it became part of Russia.

424 years have passed since the events of 1587 suggesting that the Altai nation has not quite completed the cycle of 432 years at which point it is said that the fate of the nation is decided. The nation has, however, completed the cycle of the age of wisdom. Now the issue of its future existence is being decided. At times such as these it is considered important to work with the

potential of the nation's accumulated wisdom and share it with other nations so that all those who feel so moved may unite in the initiatory processes taking place.

As far as the Altai people are concerned, it should be borne in mind that the fate of smaller nations is often tied up with the fate of other larger nations, particularly in contemporary conditions, where different nationalities living on the same territory may be politically and economically interdependent. As a result, small ethnic groups often undergo the vicissitudes of the fate of a larger nation. It is often the case that a minority nation passes its determined period (*elen chak*) and then falls into the *elen chak* of a majority nation. This has been the case in the past and is still the case being reflected in the people's worldview. This phenomenon leaves its mark on social consciousness, and as a result, on the development of the soul and the psychological well-being of the people as a whole.

The transition from one cycle to another tends to happen sporadically, taking the form of dramatic events in the public life of the nation. Events gradually ferment, ripen and finally manifest in cycles over a more or less protracted period often in the year of the snake (*d'ylan*) which occurs every twelve years. Such events may take the form of mass shifts in consciousness, upheaval, war and changes of power every twelve, twenty-four or thirty-six years. For this reason, the Altai people usually await the year of the snake with some unease. The following dates have all coincided with the year of the snake: 1905, 1917, 1929, 1941, 1953, 1965, 1977, 1989, 2001, 2013, etc. If one were to consider these dates in the light of the historical events associated with them a recurring cycle of opposition becomes apparent.

Altai Prophecy

In the seventeenth century, there lived a clairvoyant called Bor who proclaimed that the Altai people would have to survive three major events *(tuuk)* in their history. The first event is considered to have taken place in the middle of the eighteenth century when Chinese troops killed over a million Oirots and Altaians.

The second event is thought to be the civil war in the twentieth century in which approximately half the Altai nation lost their lives. According to prophecy, a third traumatic event awaits the Altai nation said to take place where two great rivers meet, the Biya and the Katun, at the very heart of Altai. This event is said to signify the beginning of the "White Era." *Jarlykchi* sometimes speak of the concept of "aversion or prevention *(tyikaru)* insurance" against traumatic or tragic experiences in one's fate. It is believed that people and nations can avert tragic events, be they political, military or personal. Dissension and the spilling of blood can be avoided by developing a new level of consciousness, a new national ideology and by acknowledging and integrating that which previously has remained unconscious.

One can only hope that Bor's prophecy of the third event in Altai history remains unfulfilled. Clairvoyants also make mistakes! May Russians, the Altai people, and other nations heed the warnings of the past and avert the foretold tragedy, together overcoming this next difficult shift. May all people, particularly those involved in politics and ideology, possess themselves of *oi* (wisdom).

Cycles in the natural world

Similarly, periods of development in the natural world are observed. In the Altai counting system this phenomenon is measured in units of 6 cycles lasting 432 years and goes back right to the very beginnings of civilization.

As a whole, historical chronology in the Altai *bilik,* or folk history, is divided into four eras *(yurgyuld'i),* and each era is marked by a certain colour (blue, black, yellow and white). Each era is in turn subdivided into epochs and periods. Just as heavenly information *(suus-aidylga)* concerning an individual's fate or purpose in life is located in the center of the soul, it is also said that information concerning the fate and purpose of a nation in the historical arena *(aidylga)* lies in the individual soul in the form of images, sounds and colours, which can be perceived and deciphered by *jarlykchi*.

The first era *(yurgyuld'i)* is called the blue *(kek,* dark blue, or *chankyr,* light blue) era. This is the ancient *(kumuran)* time, the time of the God *Ulgen* and his mother *Ak* (the Blessed White Lady). During this era Altai is referred to as *Umar-Dimar* (motherhood-fatherhood), and was covered by water. Of the times preceding the creation of life, the wise ones say, *"dyerding usti dyok tushta...* (In the time before there was land...)"* It is said that the God *Ulgen* created the land, living beings and plants. Then he created man and other beings possessed of consciousness.

The blue era is the longest of the four eras, said to have lasted for a hundred million years. This era was probably termed the blue era because at that time man had not risen above other life forms in Nature. All matters are said to have been directly ruled by God, the symbol of which is a sky blue colour. This can be interpreted in the sense that, in the beginning, the predominant and active quality in the first era was the heavenly, cosmic essence *(Kek)* and that the process of creation between earthly life and Nature had not yet been completed in its entirety. Legend has it that, apart from man, other beings possessing reason existed such as the human-like *almisi, oborotni* and sphere-headed *(bolchokbashi)* pygmies/dwarfs. Legend has it that the *Almisi* fed on animal meat and the pygmies on the meat of small children. Endowed with the power of hypnosis, they were able to speak in human tongue.

The Blue era is divided into two epochs *(enchelik).* The most ancient is referred to as *kumuran* and the following as *d'ebren*. Four geological periods are determined (*aiul*): *borax*; *d'otkon* (floods); *chaiyk* (fire, *ot*); and *d'er* (earth). In the middle of the *borax* period, huge mountain-forming processes took place. The contemporary mountains of Greater Altai were formed and there were several ice ages. During this time the pygmies died out. Different tribes migrated and replaced one another: the "giants" (*sartakpai*), "new people," the *turguti* (Turkic people, who gave the name "Altai" to this territory), *skiti* (Scythians) and Hunns.

The fire period (*turguttyn oin*) coincides with the Turkic period. In the history of the Altai people, the Turkic period is considered the most auspicious. This is reflected in myths, legends, and the words of elderly, knowledgeable people. This period saw the formation of the main clans that make up the contemporary Altai people: the *d'eleuti*, *d'elengiti*, *kumandi*, *kypchaki*, *todosh*, telesi and *irkiti*. All these original clans consider Kan Altai their *tes* (homeland).

The foundation of the folk *bilik* emerged during the blue era, including knowledge of astronomy, mathematics, geometry and biology. The Altai people revered the Eternal Sky as God on high and the God *Ulgen* as the creator of life on earth.

The second era is referred to as the black (*kara*) era. This coincides with the medieval period, the ninth to the sixteenth centuries according to the Western calendar. Black forces dominate during this whole period symbolized by Erlik. Man asserts his supremacy over Nature. He subjugates large animals of prey, and the battle between people for land, spoils and even ideas gains force. It is said that man achieved his status not only though labour, but also through competition with other human-like beings such as the *almysi* and *oborotni*. A long, dark and difficult battle for existence as supreme conscious being took place.

Legend has it that in the battle for existence, man turned to dark, "lower" energy forms for strength and so dark energies began to dominate in Kangyi above Altai encouraging the development of evil. The whole black period is exemplified by the theme of "blood" (*kan*), which severed the *elen chak* of the *telengit tribe* and continued into the following era. The beginning of the Black era is linked with the events of *d'aman chak* (dark age, age of evil) and then *achana chak* (age of hunger), which continued for more than seven centuries (Altai century 72 years) and is to a large degree connected with the Genghis (approximately ninth to the fourteenth centuries).

The elders say that in the dark era, almost every year the summer began with raids on Kan Altai by neighbours from all four sides. Of that time it is bitterly said: "Who was not lost in battle, died of starvation." At that time even women bore weapons. When women bear weapons in aid of men, the war becomes a "people's war," a "folk war." At that point the nation becomes unconquerable. Of seven centuries, six were associated with long-lasting wars, some lasting for up to ninety years with short intervals only. Legends of that time said: "They waged war for ninety years and no one fell."

To overcome the darkness of evil, the people began to place large, white icons, dedicated to Great Kan Altai, at the foremost place of the *ail (traditional Altai dwelling)*. This type of icon is called a *daiyk* in which the images of the gods are represented by different coloured ribbons. Nature is personified in the image of *Altai-Kudai*. The ancient God *Ulgen* was said to have moved "too far away" from man's soul as *Ulgen* "slept" in the eighth *Chaiykam* (heavenly vault) in *Altyn-Kazik* (the Polar Star) once man's soul had been created. Of this time it is said that *Ulgen* began associating with *Erlik* (*Ulgen Erlikle ejhik bilijher*).

The third era is the one in which we find ourselves today, the yellow (*sari*) era. The colour yellow symbolizes the simultaneous influence of good, evil and fluctuating energies in a person's consciousness.

People who have known much grief and suffering seek

kindness and justice which initiates change. On the woman's side of the *ail* (different areas of the *ail* have specific functions, including a place for men on one side and a place for women on the opposite side) the White Believers began placing a small yellow *d'aiyk* in worship of "small steppe Altai", mediator between *Altai-Kudai* and *Erlik*. Many shamans would turn to *Erlik* on the night of the old moon, interacting with the dark energies (*om*) and then during the day turn to *Ulgen* at the new moon of the rising sun, interacting with the white energies of light (*tom*).

From 1904 onwards, worship of *Erlik* gradually disappeared as *ak dyang* (the White Faith) became more established. Today, White believers only place the white *d'aiyk* in the *ail,* placing it toward the front and only worshiping Altai-Kudai. The yellow *d'aiyk* is gradually filtering out of rituals and group consciousness. Shamanism that is based on the worship of black faith also faded out as the White Faith, based on centuries of ancient wisdom and ritual took a firmer place in society.

Three epochs constitute the Yellow era. The first is the time of Oirot Khan (*oirot khan tushta*) and the Russian tsars (*Arasei kaandar*), Telengit-Altai and the Russian civilization. The second is *kurch d'ang* (sharp rule), the Soviet civilization. The third is *chookur ei,* the many coloured, motley, contemporary time.

The yellow era began at the time of Ermak's conquest of Siberia in 1583 and the formation of the independent Altai state in 1587. During the time of Oirot Khan 169 years later, external force put an end to this period in the history of the Altai nation, "*Oirot-khaan tushta altailarding uzulgen elen chagi*" .

The fourth age is the forthcoming white age. The colour white symbolizes kindness, justice, and truth (*chyndyk*), and true equality among peoples (*teng argadal*). How long the white age will last and how many epochs it will encompass remains as yet unknown. However, three periods have been indicated. The first is the period of ecology (*Yudelik*), the second is the period of air (*kei*), and the third is the period of cold (*sook*). It would seem that the three periods indicated are associated with the problems that humanity faces and which must be resolved, just as in the black age the key problems were "earth" and "blood."

The chronicle seems to suggest that time is 'speeding up'. For example, the Soviet period (*kurch d'ang*), lasted for just 72 (12x6) years. The time of the Russian state has already passed its *elen chak,* and only about fifty years remain to resolve essential issues that will tell on its future existence, such as the rejuvenation of ecology and mass consciousness.

Figure 4. "D'aiyk" by Altai Artist Choros-Gurkin

Altai faith

A brief outline of the historical development of the **Altai faith** *is given in previous chapters. This chapter concentrates on some of the basic religious concepts, rituals and symbols key to the faiths that co-exist in Altai today: Tengriism, White Faith and Shamanism.*

Three worlds and the Tree of Life

Faith in the *bilik* rests on the teachings of *Kangyi*, the cosmos and the three worlds. This knowledge is essentially common to the different belief systems in Altai although the symbolism may take different forms. In the *bilik*, knowledge of the three worlds also takes the form of the teaching of the tree of life. It is said that the teaching of the three worlds is in principle accessible to all. However, with the help of ritual *(suurum) jarlykchi* can assist others in interpreting the signs and laws of the subtle worlds.

In Altai mythology, the symbol of the world can take the form of two trees with their roots intertwined and their crowns pointing in opposite directions. It is believed that the white, light material of *Kangyi* rises upwards towards the sky (like the cream in milk) forming the "tree of life." From this white, light material, gods, white spirits *(ee)* and angels *(kegee)* are formed which represent the upper world. These are the spirits that the Altai White Believers pray to. In Altai epics it is the the 'eternal poplar' that symbolizes the world tree and marks the center of the world.

The Epic of Maadai –Kara[16] and the World Tree

The following is a short fragment from the Maadai-Kara poem performed by the master of kai singing, A. Kalkin:

Jeten airy kök talaidyŋ beltirinde
Jeti jaan köö taiganyŋ koltugunda
Jüs budaktu möŋkü terek. . .
By the shores of a blue river with seventy still waters
By the loins of seven matched black mountains,
(Grew a) hundred-branched eternal poplar. . .

Continues here from the translation into English by Ugo Mazzi:

From the side leaning towards the moon,
golden leaves fall;
from the side leaning towards the sun,
silver leaves fall.
The lowest bough has forty branches,
the highest bough has seventy branches
Under one of its boughs
a hundred mares can stay,
under yet another bough
forty rams can stay;

These two identical black eagles of mine,
guarding the deepness of the heaven
sit screeching in the middle of the iron poplar,
having built their nest.
They keep watch so that heroes
do not travel along unknown ways,
they keep guard so that heroes
do not travel along narrow ways;
their moon-like wings similar to white clouds,
my two back eagles watch over the land of the Altay.

According to the elder Kalkin the road to the lower and higher levels of the world runs up and down an eternal tree. It may be a single iron tree trunk or there may be one hundred trunks. The eternal poplar unites the upper and lower world by passing through the middle world, where humans dwell. It is believed that the world tree both brings forth and maintains life, as well as controlling human destiny. In addition to the iron poplar and other trees symbolizing the center of the world, the iron mountain also functions as the symbolic centre of the world in Altai mythology.

Teachings on the white substances that rise upwards towards the sky are set out in folk blessings (*alkysh*). Rather than being especially committed to memory a blessing naturally flows from the center of a person's soul, particularly in the case of *jarlykchi*. Numerous *alkysh* have been recorded and published in books written in the Altai language. In Altai *Alkysh* (blessings) are spoken by all, irrespective of nationality and faith for blessings strengthen the energy of morality within a person's soul.

Black substances *(om)* in *Kangyi* are heavy, (like the sediment in milk — *shilti*). The crown of the tree that represents dark substances points downwards into the lower world, the realm of *Erlik* and other dark forces. Black spirits *(shilemir)* make up the under world the teaching of which is carried in the secret rituals and mysteries *(soilodu)* of shamanism. At the current time there are no practitioners of black shamanism in Altai although observations are recorded in the work of Altai researcher, A.V. Anokhin.

The middle world which is situated on the earth's surface where humans dwell is said to be divided into the visible and the invisible. The flat territory of the middle world such as mountain valleys and plains are the realm of man and this is the visible world. Places situated either higher or lower than the flat territory such as mountains, mountain passes, ravines, gullies, and rivers are the domain of the spirits. This is the invisible world where man is a guest and should observe certain rules.

These three worlds are completely interconnected. It is impossible for one to exist without the other. Originally, the

White Believers denounced shamanism and the very existence of black spirits. To what extent such an approach corresponds to the truth and practical reality of life however, remains to be seen. An ideological transformation is currently taking place in Altai involving these two opposing ideas.

The Altai folk *bilik* has it that, together with the passing of the yellow era, where good and evil exist side by side, the coming of the white era will signal the victory of good over evil. It is said that the volume of white substance in *Kangyi* will become greater than that of dark substance. Consequently, human society will also move towards the greater good. These ideas *(ukaa)* have been set down previously by wise men and prophets *(ailatkyshchi)* like Bor, and the *kai* singers such as N. Ulagashev and A. Kalkin.

The teaching of the three worlds and the tree of life in its Altai form represents a unique understanding of the expression of God through Nature. It shares common elements with the teaching of *Kangyi*, except that the world axis in this case takes the symbol of the tree of life. This teaching is just one example of how the ideas within Tengriism and shamanism intertwine. On the one hand, the "heavenly tree" is said to connect the middle human world with the eternal sky god, *Kek Tengri*. On the other hand, the image of the world tree is used by *kams* (shamans). They traveled along its branches between the upper and lower worlds and took the souls of the dead to the base of the world tree (or mountain) where the difficult path leading to the *Erlik's* realm began.

Gods, Burkhans and the spirits of Khan-Altai

It is believed that the development of life on earth in all its diverse forms is possible only due to the energies of *Kangyi* which are said to interact in eight heavenly vaults *(chaikam)* extending out from the Earth's surface far into the cosmos. *Burkhans* play a particularly significant role in this process as sacred places where the souls of all living beings are born.

According to academics and ethnographers, in ancient times, the word *burkhan* served as the name for God in many nations of Central Asia and was eventually integrated in Altai. Evidently though, the meaning of the word in Altai mythology has changed. In the *bilik* it is a complex word comprised of two elements, *bur* and *kan*. *Bur* means liver, which is the organ particularly sensitive to the light, life-giving essence that endows one with the ability to differentiate between good and evil. *Kan* means "blood," "sacred." Therefore 'burkhan' in Altai means blood, sacred, sacred place where pure souls are born and can develop, be they human or other heavenly creatures.

Altai can be seen as a kind of cradle or incubator where earthly life, in all its diversity, can grow under the auspices of cosmic spirits. The folk teller A.G. Kalkin said, *"Tengeride segis burkhan, d'erde d'eti burkhan* (There are eight *burkhans* in the sky, and seven on the earth)."

Cult images of the *burkhans* have been preserved and are used in rituals. In the majority of cases *burkhans* are represented by different coloured ribbons and used in the *d'aiyk,* the unique White Believer icon.

The eight heavenly vaults (*chaikams*) which extend outwards from the earth's surface into the cosmos are described in the following manner:

Tuular ustyu tengeri (sky of the mountain ridge)
Ak bulut tengeri (sky of the white clouds)
Kek bulut tengeri (sky of the blue clouds)
Ak-aias tengeri (white, pure sky. *Ak-aias* means "cosmos," so
    the following categories are related to the cosmic spheres.)
Kek-aias tengeri (pure, blue sky)
Ak-kek tengeri (white-blue sky)
Agarar Kegerer tengeri (whitish-bluish sky)
(The ninety-nine sacred skies of the Galaxy; the number 99
    means "a countless number.")

Altyn Telekei tengeri (sky of the golden civilization, "Golden Cosmos")

At the peak of all the heavens is the Polar star, the "golden stake," holding the axis of *Kangyi* in place, the foundation of the spatial world. According to prophecy, in ancient times there was chaos in the world and the heavens mixed with the earth until the ruler of the heavens, God Tengri, drove the golden stake into the universe. From that point on order reigned. The heavens and the earth were held in place as the axis around which the world turns appeared.

This is the domain of the God *Ulgen*, keeper of positive energy (+) and *Mongizin-burkhan*, the mythical dragon that combines good and evil within itself and is the keeper of negative energy (-). As a result of their interaction, *Kangyi* comes into motion and the whole world is born and develops. The interaction between *Ulgen* and the dragon is all-encompassing; their energy pulsates through *Kangyi*, penetrating even the human soul. In Altai mythology, the God *Ulgen* is the Creator of life on earth whereas the dragon image is more common in China and Mongolia. *Turun-Myzykai burkhan* (the glimmering burkhan) lies in the sacred heavens of the galaxy, which directs the cosmic energies of the universe down towards the earth. In this case, parallels can be drawn with the Blue creator mentioned previously.

According to legend, in the far cosmos white spirits exist who are the protectors of peoples and nations. The constellation of the Great Bear, Ursa Major (in Altai: "Khan's children"; "seven relatives") is made up of the white spirits of *Ulgen*'s sons, from which the main tribes of the Altai people take their essence.

The Pleiades, *Mechin* or *Ak Kistar* means "white girls," and are represented in myth as the daughters of *Ulgen*. These white spirits strengthen and support the essence of goodness in human life.

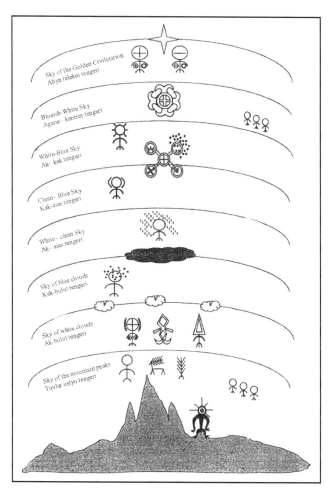

Figure 5. Gods, burkhans and spirits of Kan Altai

The sun *burkhan* is the main *burkhan* (*Kan burkhan*) and shines in "Ak-kek tengeri," impregnating the earth with its energy. The door of an *ail* (traditional Altai dwelling) faces east, meeting the first rays of the rising sun just as during prayer one faces east. In the *d'aiyk* the sun burkhan is represented by a yellow ribbon.

The moon *burkhan* (*Ai burkhan*) is situated in "*kek aias tengeri* (pure blue sky)." The moon is much more than a night luminary, reflecting the light of the sun on its surface. The moon "sorts" cosmic energies, directing them towards the earth. The moon's two companions, the Blue and White embodiers have been mentioned previously. The phases of the moon exert a huge influence on the life of man and nature. It is said that at the time of the new moon predominantly favorable energies dominate the atmosphere and so this is considered a favorable time for the birth of a child or a good time for success in other worldly affairs. In contrast, the waning moon carries more dark energies, hence important matters or decisions are put off at this time. The moon burkhan is represented in the *d'aiyk* by a pink ribbon.

The spirits of people and other living beings awaiting their earthly embodiment are located in "Pure White Sky (*ak-aias tengri*)." These spirits are then attributed to the sky burkhan and the Mother Creator (*Ene-Daichi*). These bodies determine a person's *suus*, parents, fate, and life purpose. In the *d'aiyk* the heavenly burkhan is represented by a blue or light blue ribbon.

The next atmospheric layer is called *kekshun* (violet). This is the ozone layer that protects the Earth from ultraviolet rays. Beyond this layer there is a boundary separating the warm and damp atmosphere from the cold, oxygenless layers of space.

In the layer of the sky called *kek bulut teneri* (sky of blue clouds) the condensation of water vapor takes place and the *shili burkhan* determines the processes of rain and snow above the earth's surface. This layer coincides with the sky *burkhan* and so is not represented separately in the *d'aiyk*.

It is thought that the spirit of Altai, *Altai-Kudai* and its companion *Umai-Ene* (Mother *Umai*) abide in the sky of mountain ridges, (*tuular ustu tengri*). It is in honour of these two entities that white ribbons are tied to the branches of trees and milk is sprinkled at mountain passes.

The grace of a person's life path depends on the spirit of *Altai-Kudai*. This spirit may gift an individual with extrasensory abilities. For instance, a future *jarlykchi* is normally able to see in waking or in dreaming. It is said that *Altai-Kudai* is normally seated on a white horse in white attire with a white beard. This spirit is represented in the *d'aiyk* by a white ribbon. *Altai-Kudai* is the God of honesty and fairness and has no contact with the forces of the dark. However, light and dark forces co-exist in life and so *Altai-Kudai* has a mediator in *Uch Kurbustan*. *Uch* means three. *Uch Kurbustan* is capable of creating good, evil or changeable energies. One could say that they distribute favorable white substances throughout *Kangyi* to specific people and places via angels *(kegee)* at the new moon in response to the requests and prayers of specific individuals. The representation of *Altai-Kudai* in the *d'aiyk* takes the form of square, white pieces of material with two tassles. Some Altai clans use a triangular shaped piece of material or even the image of a hare.

Abu-Burkhan is the mediator between the middle and lower worlds, residing in the lower world.

Earthly *burkhans*:

- *Tes burkhan* (burkhan of the homeland) with a sacred mountain in almost every river valley. In the *d'aiyk* this *burkhan* is represented by a green ribbon and is the only earthly *burkhan* to be represented there.
- Mother Earth burkhan – *"D'er-Ene burkhan"*
- Human burkhan – *"Kizhi burkhan"*
- White animal Burkhan – *"Ak-mal burkhan"* manifested from meat or milk substance.
- Plant burkhan – *"Arezum bukhan"*
- Bird Burkhan – *"Kush bukhan"*
- Twinkling burkhan – *"Myzyk"* or *"Mys burkhan"*

Of the seven earthly *burkhans* the main *burkhan* is the spirit of the homeland, Kan Altai itself. *Tes* (the spirit of the homeland) connects the human soul to the natural world. In Altai mythology *tes* are the benevolent spirits that existed originally in the three worlds, later becoming the homeland spirits for the

Altai clans.

The spirit of the homeland is given a second name taken from the names of the sons of *Ulgen*. The name *Bakty-Kan* is used by the Kumandy tribe, the Teles. *Karchyt-Kan* is used by the D'eleut. Kara-Kush is used by the Mundus; *D'azhil-Kan* by the Irkit; *Ed'e-Kan* by the Maiman and Telengit; *Kyrgys-Kan* by the tuba and Shortsy; *Burcha-Kan* by the Chalkandy and Baiat-d'eleut. There is also *Bai-Ulgen*, which is the name used by the larger indigenous tribes Todosh, Kypchak and Kumandy. *Ak* is used by the Kebekh and Aksuu meaning "white water", in Russian 'belovodiya', by the descendants of the Russian immigrants settling in Altai.

The first Russian immigrants called the upper reaches of the Katun River *Belovodiya* (white water), inspired by the colour of the river's water in the summer and autumn. The name "white water" is often met in ancient tales of the indigenous population. It remained only for the name to be translated into Russian as *Belovodiya* rather than the Altai *Ak suu*. The descendants of the first Russian settlers have passed the "age of consolidation" and become one of the *sook* (clans) of the native population. Adopting various aspects of local tradition and ritual the Russian settlers acquired *tes* — the spirit of the homeland — and today recount how their ancestors acknowledged Kan Altai more than two hundred years ago.

White Believers say that the spirit of the homeland consists of three elements:

- *D'er-suu*: Earth-Water, the two main elements of life and nature.
- *Dzhaiachy*: Creator, Guardian Angel, sacred clan totem animal (every clan has its own totem animal such as the deer, eagle, hare, stoat, camel, etc.)
- *Baiana*: sacred clan tree. The sacred tree is considered the ancient giver of human life. Examples are birch and pine.

The human link between *tyn* (soul), the human body, and nature lies in the fact that a person constantly receives energy in his aura from every aspect of *tes*. A person's aura, soul center, and bio-energetic field are consistently receiving pure, white, invisible substance, and in turn, radiate energy *(d'ymyru)* outwards. A person also receives life force from nature for physical nourishment and growth.

No member of any clan would ever hunt or kill their totem animal, nor would they fell their totem tree. To break this code was considered a grave crime, punishable by God. It is a direct consequence of this code that the natural world of Kan Altai has to this day been preserved in its current state. May the inhabitants of Mountain Altai remember and enforce this law so that the natural world of Altai be preserved for future generations.

Burkhans and the *d'aiyk*

It has already been said that the *d'aiyk* with its coloured ribbons *d'yalama* serves as the White Believer icon. A person praying to the *d'aiyk* may receive additional energy in their aura because the *burkhans* represented in the *d'aiyk* are the sacred places where soul energy grows and develops.

The *d'aiyk* includes five different colours, which are tied to the base (*d'ele*) with thick white thread:

The **green** ribbon symbolizes *Tes burkhan* (nature of the homeland, sacred animal and tree).

The **white** Ribbon represents the spirit of Altai, *Altai-Kudai* with *Umai-Ene*. It is a symbol of cleanliness, purity and righteousness, abundance, and success on one's life path. The white square with the two tassels represents Altai-Kudai itself, which distributes *byian* (the precious particles that emanate from all Earthly bukhans).

The **blue** ribbon symbolizes the Sky burkhan, which

maintains and deifies the initial stage of the soul's growth *(suus)*. All living beings receive *suus* from the Sky burkhan as a charge of energy for the soul center of the future child.

The **rose**-coloured ribbon symbolizes the Moon burkhan, which gives all earthly beings white, black, and clean substances for the soul's resources, for consciousness, abundance, and health.

The **yellow** ribbon symbolizes the Sun burkhan which gives vitality, development, and perfection to all living beings.

The colour black is not used in the *d'aiyk* and to White Believers, striped, dotted, red, and other dark colours are inappropriately used in folk ritual.

White Faith Pantheon in symbols (as shown in figure 6):

I   *Altyn Telekei*: "golden civilization" in the Polar Star. Keeper and key force of the whole galaxy:

    1   (+) *Ak Ulgen-Syulter*: the creator God, the one white distributor; positive energy charge (sign 31).

    2   (-) *Mongyzyn bukhan-Saksun*: dragon burkhan, negative energy charge.

    3   *Kangyi*: spirituality in *ol d'er* (the other world). (sign 31)

    a)   Movement in the layers: *suus* to Altyn Kazyk (Polar Star).

    b)   Movement in the layers: *suus* back to the earth.

    c)   In the sign for *Kangyi,* a) and b) are combined.

II   *Kudailar*: gods

    4   *Kek Dzhaiaan*: Blue creator, soul energy *(d'ymu tyn)*. Situated at the center of *Kangyi* on the axis line. Focuses the energies that give vitality to the body.

    5   *Ak Dzhaiaan*: White creator *Eerene bichyychy*, (physical embodier). Situated at the center of the solar system on

the axis line; serves as a kind of lens focusing cosmic rays for the embodiment of earthly beings.

6   *Ene-Dzhaiaan*: mother creator

7   *Uch-Kurbustan*: director, mediator between white and dark forces in *Kangyi* in the upper, middle and lower worlds.

8   *Altaidyn eezi Altai-Kudai*: Spirit of Altai, God of Altai, sometimes referred to as White burkhan.

9   *Umai ene*: Mother Umai, the "mother's womb," cohort to *Altai-Kudai*.

III *burkhans*: places of birth, development of spirits and souls

10   *Kyun Burkhans*: sun bukhan

11   *Ai Burkhans*: moon bukhan

12   *Tengeri Burkhans*: sky bukhan

13   *Ak aru tester*: white, clean spirits of the soul's homeland

14   *Tes Bukhan*: spirit of the homeland

15   *Abu Bukhan*: mediator between white *Altai-Kudai* and dark *Erlik*

IV   *Kegee*: servants to Altai-Kudai, guardian angels

16   *Agaru-tyn*: holy soul

17   *D'er Ene*: mother earth

18   *Ulu-Kegen*: great knowledge

19   *Karlyk Ene*: mother of divination

20   *Tarun-d'aiyk*: *burkhan* images

21   *Bakty-Sonko*: protector of the homeland

22   *Tep-Kara*: judge

23   *Shan-D'ime*: protector of children

24   *Syut Kel*: milky, healing lake

25   *Mai Sanai*: motherhood

26   *Mandy Shire*: fatherhood

V   *Eeler*: spirits

   27   *Tuu Eezi*: spirit of the mountain

   28   *Suu Eezi*: spirit of the river

   29   *Ot Eezi*: spirit of the fire

   30   *Agash Eezi, Shangyr*, etc.: spirit of the forest

VI   *Temdek*: Signs

   31   *Kangyi*: common spirituality of *Ak Ulgen*

   32   *Kairakon bash*: gods

Figure 6 Cult signs for gods, burkhans and spirits of *kangyi*

33 *Myurgyuyul*: prayer
34 *Suda*: the Milky Way, axis of *Kangyi*
35 Vibrational direction, "shock absorber" of *Kangyi's* axis.

VII *Sakpuzyndar*: protective amulet
    36 *Altai-Kudai, Umai-Ene, Uch-Kurbustan*

VIII. *Shilemirler*: dark spirits
    37 *Erlik*
    38 *Kara tester*: dark spirits of the souls of the homeland
    39 *Kermester, kyuryum*: demons
    40 *Cherdik*: mask, *kuulgazyn* (mysticism)
    41 the direction of honest, cleansed souls
    42 direction of sinful souls

Angels

Kegee (angels) serve God in the parallel worlds. In the middle world, God's direct servants are *jarlykchi*, imbued with astral power. It is thought that angels give spiritual strength to people and other living beings. Their number in the White Faith is not known for certain as much has been forgotten. The main angel (*kegee*) is *Ot-ene* (mother fire). It is said: "*odus alti bashtu Ot-ene* (thirty-six-headed Mother of fire)." The number varies and could be 33 or 42. So far twenty-five have been specifically determined. The names of elements serving black magic are neither named nor worshiped by White Believers. It goes without saying that the positive energy and benefit to man of every *burkhan* and angel goes beyond the limits of the function mentioned above. Any person who believes can call on an angel. The angel they choose depends on many factors such as their age, time of birth, whether it is new moon or old moon and the specific nature of their concern or ailment.

In the past, the angels' names were associated with a specific date. Some ancient pagan dates are now observed at the new moon. Here follow examples from 1999:

17 January (new moon): *Ene Jaian* (Mother Creator). The cult sign is a square with creation rays and the sign for the soul at the center.

25 January: *Karlik-Ene* (Mother Diviner) (with four ears)

28 January: *Burcha Kan* develops the talent of masters

18 February: *Kocho Kan* brings loved ones together

29-30 February: *Ak Taru* celebration of "white creation," like Mardi gras', directs the people's culture

19 March: *Mai Teere* (most profound understanding) protects the soul of the mother.

29 March: *Dyer Ene* (Mother Earth) oversees the reawakening of nature and the beginning of spring. Sign is a circle with seven layers and four sectors. Old New Year.

01 April: *Tabi-Taru* (creativity – morality) holds jokes and calls forth joyful laughter.

18 April: *Dara Chechen* (the fall of harshness) brings family members and friends closer together.

28 April: *Shan Dime* (little bell) Mother Umai's helper. Protects the souls of babies, young animals and shoots.

04 May: *Tep-Kara* (judge) decides where to send the soul of a deceased person, to leave it in the *tes* (homeland), or send it to

	tami (the underworld).
?????	*Dalkyn* Celebration of the first storm when lightning fire cleanses *Kangyi* of the *suus* that have served their time and dark substances.
26 June:	*Agaru-Tyn* Celebration of the "holy soul," similar to the Trinity in the Christian calendar, angel of the celebration of the "green leaves."
28 June:	*Nogon Taru* (blue creation) brings calm to shepherds in the high mountain meadows.
15 July:	*Chaiik Kan* (flood) provides safety, the ability to swim to all people and other beings.
28 July:	*Syut Kyol* (milky lake) rejuvenates the sick at *arjhanax* (sacred springs).
15 August:	*Bakhti-Sonko* (protector) day of the protector of Altai from encroachment by enemies; develops love for the homeland and *uide* (the family home).
19 August:	*Tulaan Kan* (ancestral land) provides the maturing of the harvest, plant life, crops and herbs.
12 September:	*Ulu kegen* (great wisdom) inspires striving towards the *bilik*, knowledge and wisdom, particularly in young people.
23 September:	*Ot Iaan* (fire spirit) reminds people and animals of autumn work in *kuski kaandar* (Indian summer).
12 October:	*Tarun nama* (minister of creation) prepares man and nature for the forthcoming winter. Parents prepare

	dowries, presents for loved ones, and the elderly make their wills.
24 October:	*Ak Tyn* (White soul) angel of the "Yellow leaves" festival. People strengthen their aura with prayers in preparation for the forthcoming winter.
10 November:	*Mandi shire* (mythical hero) reminding everyone of the role of the father in the family.
10 December:	*Targun Kan* (sacred creation) develops creative thinking and the search for understanding, to find the new, and perfect the old. People gather together to listen to folk tellers, guess riddles, exercise their wit, and compose new songs.
20 December:	*Ulu Dargun* (the great judge) angel of forgiveness, confession (*dalbaru*), cleansing of taboos committed before *Altai-Kudai*.

Prayer *Ailatkysh* & Blessing *Alkysh*

Much of the Altai spiritual philosophy is contained in Altai prayers and blessings. The more deeply one is acquainted with prayer - *ailatkysh* - the more effective one's spiritual practice becomes and the firmer the qualities of faith, kindness, and self confidence become instilled in one's being.

To read a blessing - *alkysh* in the Altai language - one should determine one's intentions in order to achieve one's goal. When making a blessing, one turns towards the east where the sun rises, and then to the peak of a sacred mountain, or to the *daiyk*, making a small bow. Men remove their hats or other headwear and with the right palm stroke their head several times from the crown to the forehead and women stroke their hair forwards or push it behind their ears with both hands bending their head. In cult symbols this action is indicated by a rhombus (figure 6, sign 32).

Below is an example of an Altai blessing:

> Lord God Altai! Spirit of Altai! Precious elements! Give your blessing! May no dark substance curse my path with obstacles. Help me to fulfill my purpose. White substance, give your strength, pure substance, give the consciousness necessary in order to ... (personal intention follows). May the spirit of kindness fill our hearts, God Altai, Spirit of Altai! Amen!

The expression **Amin'** originated from the prayer of the ancient Altai Turks: "*Adasu, uuldyng, agaru tynnyng adyna min!* (Sit on the horse of the father, the son, and the holy spirit!)" Nowadays, in place of *Adina Men!*, we say, *Chok[17]!*, which means, "I worship, revere and bow before you!"

Blessings are required in order to strengthen the energy of the soul and its morality with lofty particles and kind intentions. A blessing has power when one feels a light movement on the nape of the neck or other part of the body. Any individual can say a blessing, irrespective of belief, world view, nationality, or education, for ultimately, God is one. Of course, a blessing should always come from one's very soul, where one's motivations and pure and honest. In the Altai faith it is believed that one's dark thoughts and motivations eventually turn back on one.

Blessings expressing good intentions are made at group prayer meetings, usually held at the new moon before mid-day in the morning sunlight. A blessing may be made later than mid-day if the sun is high in the sky. Aura cleansing rituals using fire *(alas)* are carried out at the new moon also. Various things may be burnt, including heather, wax, oil and animal fats, such as lard although the fat from pig or goat is not used. No prayers are carried out by White Believers after dusk and particularly at night because it is believed that there is more dark material in *Kangyi* at these times.

Actions of worship *(d'albaru)* to *Kan Altai* and Nature can be conducted every month, but only at the time of the new moon. It is preferable to find a place high up in a sacred mountain avoiding the peak. White ribbons or ribbons in other colours of the *d'aiyk* may be tied to certain trees such as cedar, birch, or larch. The fir is avoided. Milk may be sprinkled in offering and a small fire lit. Previously untouched food may be placed in the fire as an offering.

Group prayer meetings are usually held at the beginning of summer at the white full moon in June (the month of little heat) at the celebration called *'dajhil bur'*, "green leaves". The 'green leaves' event coincides with the ancient Russian pagan holiday of the Trinity: Whitsun. Celebrations can be held a few days earlier depending on the weather, but they must be held before the waning moon. A second group prayer meeting is held in the autumn, in the month of October at the celebration *sari byur* (yellow leaves) and again this is held at the time of the white full moon. The purpose of both prayers is the same: to cleanse and strengthen one's own aura and that of family and loved ones.

After the consecration with fire *(alas)*, the *daiyk* takes on a specific energy field *(kachaa)*. During prayer, this energy is transferred to the aura of the worshipper and protects their body from dark substances in the external world.

Blessings made during prayer do not necessarily have to take poetic form, nor do they necessarily have to be spoken aloud. The names of Gods are pronounced: *Altai-Kudai, Ak-burkhan,* and *Uch-Kurbustan*, Spirit of Altai, and *Umai-Ene,* and the corresponding angels. The person making the prayer usually says their name and *sook* (kin, clan), *tes* (spirit of the homeland) and then expresses their pure intention.

Altai magic

Altai magic *(tarmalga)* has existed since ancient times. The word *tarmalga* includes the semantics of sorcery, wizardry, witchcraft, magic, superstitions *(suurumd'y)*, predictions *(belge)*, signs, omens *(yrym)* and incantations *(emit)*.

The ritual objects that are now held in various museums in Altai are covered in symbols that speak their own language. From these signs one can discern that white and black magic existed side by side in *Kan Altai* since ancient times. They represented the polarities in all that is. The symbol for white magic is a leather milk vessel *(bulkunchuk)* used for holding milk that is sprinkled during prayer. The sign for black magic is a mask *(cherdik)*, which can be explained by the fact that a person loses their true identity when they practice black magic, conducting rituals *(suurumy)*, in the name of *sunye* (the soul of a deceased who has linked into dark energies *(om)*).

Cult signs can be found on such objects as flint stones. (See figure 9). On flint stones used in white magic, the morning star was shown, and on those used in black magic, either the evening star or two masks were depicted. Some signs appear on both, such as the triangle symbolizing the spirit of *Kan Altai*.

The God of Altai is depicted by a six-petaled peony. The spirits of the morning and evening star are depicted by five-petaled flowers. Symbols of Great and Small Altai are depicted by triangles.

Ritual

One of the most important actions of a sorcerer is considered to be the banishment of the spirit of illness *(albychy)*, or demons *(kyuryum)* from a person's soul. A *kyuryum* may settle in the soul center *(ezek)*. The illness *(kyuryum)* can cause a person to be guileful, cruel, and merciless, causing harm to family and others. The *jarlykchi* considers such a person to be the victim of dark energies.

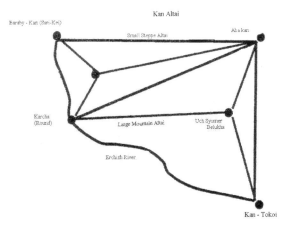

Kan Altai

Baraby - Kan (Sari-Kei)

Abakan

Small Steppe Altai

Karcha (Round)

Large Mountain Altai

Uch Syumer Belukha

Erchish River

Kan - Tokoi

Figure 7. Symbol of Kan Altai from the Erchish River dating back to the Middle Ages.

Figure 8. Symbol of the ancient homeland.

The dark energy is said to have become materially manifest in his soul, destroying the white energy of kindness. If the sorcerer is unable to banish *kyuryum* from a person's soul, he may request the assistance of a more powerful *jarlykchi*.

Rituals for healing the sick are carried out between the eighth and fifteenth day after the new moon early in the day when there is most white substance *(tom)* in *Kangyi*. During the ritual the *jarlykchi* will say a blessing *(alkysh)* or incantation *(emit)*. The sick person may be given a protective amulet made by the *jarlykchi* himself to be carried on one's person for *(sakpuzyn)* protection from dark energies and influences.

It was considered that dark energies gained in strength during the old moon, particularly on the last day of the waning moon, *aidyng arazy,* at *kyzyl enir* (literally "red evening") and at nightfall. A *kam* would say a *soilodu* (incantation) over the body of the sick. He would make the person another sort of amulet called a *kandokoi,* a "black" amulet for protection from other dark forces.

During the ritual a *kam* would use a drum *(tunur)*, and *kermezhek*, a ritual object symbolizing images of the *kam's* parents on the maternal and paternal line for six generations. It was considered that a *kepmezhek* embodied the images of the *kam's* ancestors thereby protecting the *kam* and his family from accidents, ill-spoken words, and the evil eye. They were also used in divination. Every *kermezhek* had its own specific sphere of influence—over hunting, healing people, protecting the herd, children's health, etc. During a séance the *kam* would call the name of one of his ancestors to assist him. The handle of the drum would be the image of the head ancestral *kam* (*byudyuk*).

There are at the present time no *kams* in Altai who truly serve the dark force, worshiping *Erlik*, as there were in days gone past. *Jarlykchi*, who use white energies in their rituals, use *archyn*, heather and the *d'aiyk*.

A person practicing Altai magic might, for example, be called to carry out a ritual after a death. A clairvoyant or spirit-seer *(kesmekchi)* is invited to the home of the deceased. When a person dies the thread connecting *syulter* (+) and *saksun* (-) is broken. A *kesmekchi* is able to see the separated *syulter* which is the soul of the deceased, called *yyuzut*. The yyuzut communicates with the *kesmekchi*, expressing its last wishes before departing. It is said that on the seventh day after death, the *yyuzut* returns home to collect certain belongings needed in the after world. The *yyuzut* collects the spirit of the personal belongings and accepts refreshments.

The *kesmekchi* carries out the ritual of making offerings to the *yyuzut*. This ritual takes place early on so-called "red evening," with offerings being made from an earthenware bowl (*yamockhi*). Food is placed in the bowl, alcohol is sprinkled on the ground and crockery is smashed while the following words are spoken: "Don't look back, look ahead to where you have been called. Don't hang on to your home and family!"

In recent years *kesmekchi* have begun discussing the fact that *yyuzut* are leaving resentfully. They fear the bright electric lights and noise which make it difficult for them to enter their home. As a result there are more accidents and increasing general negativity. It would be well for the living to listen to the '*yyuzuts*' and revive the practice of the ancient ritual, '*surum*'. In accordance with the ritual, the home should be kept quiet and the door left open or ajar on an unlit room.

On the seventh day the spirit of milk leaves the human body. (Christians acknowledge this process on the ninth day. The spirit of meat leaves the body on the fortieth day.

The angel *Tep-Kara* judges the *yyuzut* placing it on a blade of grass (see chapter Spirituality and the Soul). If the blade bends, the soul is concluded to have become 'heavy' as a result of having broken the laws of nature during carnation. In this case, the soul is sent to the underworld to be cleansed. The period of cleansing in the underworld depends on the seriousness of the negative actions committed during carnation and can last for generations.

After the fortieth day, the *yyuzut* should never again return to the family home or pursue loved ones. The soul of an innocent person who has been murdered may pursue or haunt the killer wherever he might be. The soul of such a victim acts mostly on the killer's *d'yugel* (brain matter), his thinking *(sanal),* his consciousness *(shyunyu),* and may appear to him in dreams.

White Believers did not originally mark the passing of a year after death so as not to trouble the soul of the deceased unnecessarily or call the soul back to the family home. Should the deceased appear in a relative's dream, a *jarlykchi* might be called to conduct the *suurum* (ritual), which aims to separate the soul of the deceased from the relative's consciousness. *Alas* (the fire cleansing ritual) is carried out around the relative's aura, through the house and *d'aiyk* and the words of *emit* are spoken. Alternatively, the relative may make a gift to friends or cook them a meal, saying the name of the deceased and asking that the soul rest in peace in its own world.

Figure 9 White Faith flintstone decorated with cult symbols.

Altai-Kudai is symbolised by a six-petaled peony and the spirits of the morning and evening stars are symbolised by five-petaled flowers. The symbols of Large and Small Altai are represented by triangles.

Afterword

Through the work you have just read, Nikolai Andreevich Shodoev invites us to consider the spiritual wisdom of the Altai indigenous culture beyond the popular theme of the shaman and shamanism. In many cases, the shamans as we know them from ethnographic record no longer practice. For this reason, there is a tendency to associate 'shamanic cultures' with the past. Yet through the notion of the *bilik* Nikolai Andreevich has succeeded in building a bridge that carries Altai traditional knowledge of the soul, moral values and nature into the future. As Rustam writes in Chapter One, the *bilik* "simultaneously incorporates ancient wisdom while embracing contemporary science. The content of the *bilik* is constantly being re-assimilated philosophically and serves as a prism, through which solutions to contemporary problems may be found". Nikolai Shodoev's work on the *bilik* has particular significance at a time when traditional knowledge is more widely becoming acknowledged as essential not only to the integrity of indigenous cultures themselves, but also to the wider community in its search for sustainable values.

It has been a privilege to work with Nikolai Andreevich, to experience the gravity of his insights and his passion for the true wisdom of the Altai world. Perhaps on reading the English translation of *Altai Spiritual Wisdom: Altai Bilik* the reader will agree that the Altai *bilik*, as Nikolai Andreevich has stated, indeed "reveals a profound relationship to life, a deep understanding of natural energies and rhythms and a keen feeling for the dramatic contradictions of our time."

Nikolai Andreevich continues his research and writing. He has recently published a new book *An Altai Philosophy* (available in Russian at the Museum in Mendur Sokkon village). He seeks collaborators to explore the connections among physics, cosmology and traditional knowledge as it is encoded in various forms of cultural heritage.

Joanna Dobson, 2011

Translator and sponsors

Joanna Dobson author of the Altai Pilgrim website, has been living and working in Altai as researcher and translator for the past eight years. She writes within the context of the growing

Shodoev and translator Joanna
Dobson by Jodi Frediani

interest in indigenous cultures and spiritual cultural values that is being witnessed among academics, environmentalists and leading edge spiritual figures alike; she describes this shared path of enquiry that is emerging in the western world as 'the most significant pilgrimage of our time'.

'Evolution is inherent in the Earth. The indigenous people who are listening to the Earth intently know where that call must take us. Therefore, supporting indigenous initiatives is an effective way of creating a buffer zone between the depths of the Earth and the depths of the Sky'. Based on these principles, the *Altai Pilgrim Friendship Circle* supports a number of small-scale, grass-root projects together with indigenous friends and colleagues.

Altai Pilgrim Website http://altaipilgrim.wordpress.com

'Spiritual Wisdom from the Altai Mountains *Altai Bilik'* was sponsored by Altai Pilgrim Friendship Circle, Sacred Earth Network and Dream Change

Dream Change is dedicated to shifting personal and global consciousness and inspiring actions that transform the world. This is accomplished through written materials and books; workshops and presentations; sacred expeditions and gatherings with indigenous peoples; community programs and trainings in the US and abroad; specialized environmental projects and those that educate about, and preserve, traditional cultures and earth-wise values. Dream Change has partnered with and supported diverse indigenous groups. Its workshops and trainings cut to the heart of cultural and environmental issues by applying the wisdom of original peoples to shift the consciousness of societies that are responsible for global imbalance. www.dreamchange.org

Significant Dates in the History
of the Altai People

1207: The lands of Altai are conquered by Genghis khan's oldest son becoming a part of the Golden Horde.

1500: First reference to 'Altai' in Russian written sources.

1587: Altai clans (*sook*) unite against Mongolian supremacy and refuse to pay tribute (*kalan*). Their own kaan is appointed.

1635: Separate Oirot clans (immediate neighbours of the Altai clans) are united under the **Jungar khanate**.

1720: Old Believers begin settling in the Uimon valley (Ust'-Koks region) Altai.

1756: **Southern Altai group becomes a part of Russia** looking for protection from oppression by the Jungarian clans. (The northern Altai clans had become a part of Russia previously).

1830: The first Russian Orthodox missionary camp in Gorny Altai was opened by archimandrite Makary (Glukharev) in 1830. In the nearly 90 years of its existence, **the Altai Spiritual Mission** opened more than 40 churches and houses of prayer, two monasteries and the Biysk Catechist School.

1831: Ulala town is formed (future Gorno-Altaisk).

1889: The eighth century "Orkhon inscriptions," were discovered in the Orkhon Valley in Mongolia containing many references to **Tengri**. In the *Secret History of the Mongols* (written 1227), Genghis-Khan began all his declarations with the words, "By the will of Eternal Blue Heaven."

1904 May: Large-scale prayer meeting to the **White Burkhan Messiah** held by the Altai people in the **Tereng Valley, Ust' Khan region**. The prayer meeting was forcibly broken up by the authorities. *'White Faith'*, *'Ak dyang'*, a strand of Altai faith; worship of the one heavenly God, the White Burkhan; and the expected return of Oirot-khan as a national hero and Savior. At the very beginning of the twentieth century White Faith underwent a resurgence in the form of a new national religion in counterbalance to shamanism, which had become outmoded and this resurgence is referred to as Burkhanism.

1919:   Soviet power established in Altai

1922:   The **Oirot Autonomous Region** was formed at the centre of Oirot-Tura town (now Gorno-Altaisk).

1926:   Roerich began his **Trans-Himalayan expedition** through Altai.

1929:   First excavations of **Pazyryk kurgans** carried out by Russian archaeologist Rudenko.

1937:   New administrative unit **'Altai Territory'** formed.

1948:   Oirot autonomous region renamed Gorno-Altaiskii region and Oirot-Tura town renamed Gorno-Altaisk.

1991:   **Mountain Altai** ceases to be a part of the Altai Territory gaining status of Republic and subject of the Russian Federation.

1992:   Mountain Altai renamed 'Altai Republic'.

1993-4:   Excavations prevented by local population in Karakol valley but continued on the Ukok Plateau. Excavation of the so-called 'Ice-Maiden'.

Endnotes

1. *Dmitriev A. N.* - Institute of Geology Siberian Branch Russian Academy of Science. Conducts field research in the Altai Republic related to anomalous geomagnetic fields etc.

2. *Sartakpai* - mythological giant connected with legends surrounding the rocks of the Katun river that runs through the Altai Republic.

3. *Oirot-khaan* - a composite figure constructed from memories of the Jungarian khans. The Altai tribes had been ruled under the Junagrian khanate 1635-1758. The rule of Oirot-khaan is said to have been a Golden Age of justice and happiness. Oirot-khaan did not die but rather left for the east promising one day to return with the sun and restore his kingdom. Later associated with the Ak-Burkhan Messiah of the White Faith in the early twentieth century.

4. *Kudai* - The Persian name given to Tengri in the middle ages. A deity. Also, *Altai-Kudai*. Sometimes it is used in relation to natural objects and phenomena, such as Sun *Kudai*, Moon *Kudai*, and Mountain *Kudai*. Nonetheless, presently a monotheistic understanding of this word prevails. In the 19th century the Orthodox missionaries adopted this word as an Altaian equivalent of "God" in their translations of the Bible and prayers.

5. *Kalkin* - born in 1925 in the Ulagan region of Altai, was endowed with the gift of '*Kai*'. '*Kai*' is considered the core of the Altai culture as the epic texts performed by the '*kaichi*' — '*Kai* singer' blend Altai history, spiritual and material culture. Throughout his life Kalkin became renowned for his talents in performing Altai 'Kai' in the traditional style of throat-singing accompanied by the drone of the traditional wooden, two-stringed 'topshur'. Kalkin's name has become legend not only for his skills as a '*kaichi*' but also for his

immense gift of wisdom. However, due to the political climate of his day he was accused of being superstitious, religious and a liar. His wisdom and knowledge were left unrecognised by the state, despite the fact that he could have contributed a great legacy to both to science and to his people.

6. *Kai* - Altai word for the performance of epic works in the form of throat-singing. 'Kaichi' means 'singer of kai'. At one time, kai was widely diffused amongst the Eurasian peoples; but under the influence of progressive-urbanized civilization began to fade and become lost, preserved only in certain areas such as Altai. Amongst some Turkic peoples there is the opinion that kai is a divine gift, the word of God.

7. *Nicholas Roerich* (9.10.1874 – 13.12. 1947), was a Russian painter, philosopher, scientist, writer, traveller, and public figure. Roerich was initiator of an international pact for the protection of artistic and academic institutions and historical sites (Roerich's Pact) and a founder of an international movement for the defence of culture. In the West, the Roerich family is perhaps best known for the Altai-Himalayas expedition (1924-1928) which ran through Sikkim, Kashmir, Ladakh, China (Sintzian), Russia, Siberia, Altai, Mongolia and Tibet, unstudied areas of Trans Himalayas. During the expedition the books "Heart of Asia" and "Altai-Himalayas" were written and about five hundred paintings were created, in which the artist portrayed the beauty and panorama of the expedition itinerary (series "Himalayas", "Maytreya", "Sikkim's Path", "His country", "The Teaches of the East").

8. *White Faith, 'Ak D'yang'* – 'Ak' – 'White', 'D'yang' – 'law', 'faith'.

9. *Burkhanism* - Confusion sometimes arises between the terms White Faith and Burkhanism. 'Burkhanism' is the term used in academic literature to refer to the movement in the early

twentieth century that culminated in the sorry events of 1904. (See timeline) Burkhanism was a social, political phenomenon as much as it was a spiritual one. The word 'burkhan' was chosen because the highest deity was renamed from 'Ulgen' to 'Altai-Kudai', 'Ak Burkhan'. The Altai people refer to their faith as 'Ak Jang', rather than 'Burkhanism'.

10. *Gumilev L.N. (1912-1992)* Russian historian & anthropologist. Gumilev wrote on the history of the Turkic people. To describe his ideas on the genesis and evolution of the ethnos, Gumilev introduced the concept of "passionarity", which may be explained as the level of vital energy and power characteristic of any given ethnic group.

11. *Anokhin A.V.-* Early twentieth century researcher of Altai shamanism; of Russian descent. Composer, music historian, ethnographer. Recorded musical arts in Altai, Tuvan, Mongolia.

12. *Nikolai Ulagashev* was born March 17th, 1861. The works recorded by 'kaichi' N.Ulagashev constitute the main fund of Altai oral culture known today. He died in 1946.

13. *Jarlykchi* - a term denoting spiritual specialists connected with Burkhanism. Also denotes a respected foreteller or wisdom keeper. May offer healing and spiritual guidance.

14. *Noosphere – for Wikipedia introduction to the Noosphere see:*http://en.wikipedia.org/wiki/Noosphere

15. *Katun River* – Main river running through the Altai Republic. Originates in the Katun glaciers on the southern slopes of Belukha Mountain. The river is 688 km long.

16. *Maadai-Kara* is one of the most vivid examples of the Altai epic in which the hero Kogudei-Mergen saves his people from the evil conqueror Kara-Kula. The epic was written down by the storyteller A. G. Kalkin who heard it from his father. The sacred poplar 'Bai-Terek', the hero's steed, and the hero himself, perform feats in three worlds, the underworld, the visible world of Altai, and then in the upper world

as they ascend to heaven. *Maadai-Kara* can be described as the spiritual apex of Altai, which like an everlasting, live-giving spring, blesses and satiates the entire atmosphere, reviving with its animating breath the deepest layers of the culture's roots. 'When the epic is performed it literally stuns its listeners. The unique specialness of Altai is experienced through a feeling of deepest unity, not only with each other, but with nature, and with Earth's heroic past; the listeners feel their involvement and a sense of responsibility both for the past and the future of the Earth.' M.Y.Shishin

17. *Chök!* - According to Radlov [1893, t. III, p. 2034] this word means genuflection, kneeling. Baskakov [1947, p.180] describes it as: an exclamation during sprinkling for idols. Used in ritual context and occurs in shamanic texts.

Moon Books invites you to begin or deepen your encounter with Paganism, in all its rich, creative, flourishing forms.